The Operations Manager's Toolbox

The Operations Manager's Toolbox

Using the Best Project Management Techniques to Improve Processes and Maximize Efficiency

Randal Wilson

Vice President, Publisher: Tim Moore
Associate Publisher and Director of Marketing: Amy Neidlinger
Executive Editor: Jeanne Glasser
Editorial Assistant: Pamela Boland
Operations Specialist: Jodi Kemper
Marketing Manager: Megan Graue
Cover Designer: Chuti Prasertsith
Managing Editor: Kristy Hart
Project Editor: Elaine Wiley
Copy Editor: Cheri Clark
Proofreader: Jess DeGabriele
Indexer: Erika Millen
Compositor: Nonie Ratcliff
Manufacturing Buyer: Dan Uhrig

© 2013 by Randal Wilson
Publishing as FT Press
Upper Saddle River, New Jersey 07458

FT Press offers excellent discounts on this book when ordered in quantity for bulk purchases or special sales. For more information, please contact U.S. Corporate and Government Sales, 1-800-382-3419, corpsales@pearsontechgroup.com. For sales outside the U.S., please contact International Sales at international@pearsoned. com.

Company and product names mentioned herein are the trademarks or registered trademarks of their respective owners.

Printed in the United States of America

First Printing December 2012

ISBN-10: 0-13-306468-9
ISBN-13: 978-0-13-306468-1

Pearson Education LTD.
Pearson Education Australia PTY, Limited
Pearson Education Singapore, Pte. Ltd.
Pearson Education Asia, Ltd.
Pearson Education Canada, Ltd.
Pearson Educación de Mexico, S.A. de C.V.
Pearson Education—Japan
Pearson Education Malaysia, Pte. Ltd.

Library of Congress Cataloging-in-Publication Data

Wilson, Randal Paul, 1961-
 The operations manager's toolbox : using the best project management techniques to improve processes and maximize efficiency / Randal Wilson.—1 Edition.
   pages cm
 Includes bibliographical references and index.
 ISBN 978-0-13-306468-1 (hbk. : alk. paper)—ISBN 0-13-306468-9 (hbk. : alk. paper)
 1. Project management. I. Title.
 HD69.P75W5595 2012
 658.4'04—dc23
                              2012037457

I would like to dedicate this book to my wife, Dusty, and sons, Nolan, Garrett, and Carlin, for their support and patience through this project.

I would also like to dedicate this book to my parents, Paul and Maxine, and my entire family for their love, support, and encouragement throughout my career.

Contents

About the Author

Randal Wilson, MBA, PMP serves as Visiting Professor of Project Management, Keller Graduate School of Management, at the Elk Grove, CA DeVry University campus. His teaching style is one of addressing Project Management concepts using not only academic course guidelines and text, but includes in-depth discussions in lectures using practical application from industry experience.

Mr. Wilson is currently Operations and Project Manager at Parker Hose and Fittings. He is responsible for five locations across Northern California and Nevada, as well as project management of redesigns and renovation of existing facilities and construction of new facilities.

Mr. Wilson was formally in the telecommunications industry as Senior New Product Introduction Engineer at REMEC, Inc., Senior New Product Introduction Engineer with Spectrian Corp. and Associate Design Engineer with American Microwave Technology. He also served as Senior Manufacturing Engineer at Hewlett Packard.

He is a certified Project Management Professional (PMP) of the Project Management Institute. He acquired an MBA with concentration in General Operations Management from Keller Graduate School of Management of DeVry University in Fremont, CA and a Bachelor of Science in Technical Management with concentration in Project Management from DeVry University in Fremont, CA.

Preface

Organizations grow and thrive based on their response to a competitive environment within a particular market. The success of an organization in how it responds to market demand is largely dependent on how the organization is structured and managed. Today's world of Internet-based e-commerce allows for a broader and potentially worldwide market base requiring faster response in managerial decision processing. The knowledge, skill, and experience within management will dictate the speed and quality of managerial decision processing and the competitive advantage it will afford the organization.

It's the knowledge and skill managers have that establish how managerial processes are developed and implemented, and what effect these processes will have in the overall operation. Much like people who use tools to perform their work, their success is largely dependent on knowing what tools to use, when to use them, and how to use them to accomplish a desired goal. Managers can also have tools that will help develop processes to manage their department more effectively and efficiently.

Project managers have used several specific tools designed to manage various components of a project to ensure that the project is completed by the appropriate staff, on budget, on schedule, and delivering a quality product or service. Project management tools used for developing processes to manage resources and other levels of management, communications, budget and schedule, supply chain, process improvement, facilities, and waste as well as risk management can also be applied to operations management, having proved to be very effective in maximizing efficiency, productivity, and problem resolution. This gives managers more power and confidence not only in managing and completing their responsibilities, but also in offering efficient ways to improve the culture of management and how the organization conducts business.

Organizations are continually looking to improve competitive advantage, typically through product improvement and production efficiency, but this book offers the manager tools to make improvements not related to product, but that can result in similar improvements in the organization's competitive advantage. These tools can be implemented in small businesses to very large corporations with locations all over the world, as well as organizations such as government, educational, and nonprofits. These tools can be used by operations managers as well as executive management and lower or mid-level managers because they are effective in all areas of managerial responsibility.

Managers can now have their own tools that will change how they approach managerial responsibilities. When managers implement these tools and witness their usefulness firsthand, this will result in stronger and more confident management resources, creating an advanced and technical managerial base of assets within the organization. It will be these highly effective managers who will create a culture of managerial decision processes, and based on these tools can help organizations turn the tides of competitive advantage to their favor. Managers can now make a bigger difference than ever in being effective by having the right tools and knowing when and how to use them.

Introduction

Realities of Managing

Organizations can be made up of anything from small two- or three-person operations to very large corporations having several divisions broken up into departments with thousands of employees managed by several layers of management, all sharing similar characteristics. These characteristics can include processes performed for a specific objective, operating and overhead expenses, schedules, capital equipment management, and human resource management. These are just a few characteristics that are typical in an organization, but they represent areas that will need to be managed and will likely see problems at some point.

When organizations are first established, the founders and executive staff will largely be responsible for establishing policies and procedures that set the stage for how the organization will be run and the direction it will go. Managers will then be hired to oversee procedures being completed and policies being followed within the organization.

This is much like a captain steering a ship. The captain will understand a course that was laid out and will have the skills, tools, and experience to maneuver the vessel to reach its destination. If the manager is seen as the captain over the department or division, the manager must understand the course, which would be the processes that are carried out to accomplish a desired goal, and then the manager must have the knowledge, skills, and tools to effectively steer the department toward the desired objective. This not only requires the department to be pointed in the right direction, but also requires the manager to know how to make adjustments to steer the department and keep it on track.

The question is, Does the manager have the knowledge and tools needed to make *necessary adjustments to keep the department on its course?*

Project Management Tools for Operations Management

Much like operations managers, project managers have several areas to monitor and control in steering a project in the right direction. Projects have several of the same characteristics as a department within a functional organization. They have work packages or tasks that are performed one time and that must be completed to accomplish the project objective. Departments have work packages called processes that they perform on an ongoing basis, such as human resource management or resource and material scheduling, and that must be completed to accomplish the objective that the department was designed for. Project managers are typically under pressure to create a well-organized, highly efficient, streamlined flow of processes that will define a particular project. Managers will also have processes being carried out within a department designed to produce a desired output. It is this connection between how project managers approach managing these processes and how operation managers approach them that reveals project management tools that can be used in operations management.

Project managers, in most cases, approach a project looking at every aspect of work that needs to be done, as well as all of the resources required to accomplish the objective. This is an eyes-wide-open approach, looking at every aspect of the project as seen for the first time. Because operations managers see their processes every day, they can overlook areas that appear normal but in reality are causing problems. Managers who step back to view their department as if seeing it for the first time might discover some obvious improvements that can be made. This book will give managers tools and perspectives that can be used to unveil hidden problems and areas that can be improved that may not be readily visible to the manager.

In some cases, just looking at things with a different perspective can in itself be a powerful tool. This can reveal areas over which the manager does not have much control and which therefore warrant investigation into setting up monitoring systems to gather information about how much and what types of controls might need to be implemented. This is why project managers will see things that operations managers might miss, simply because they are not used to looking for them. This book is designed to have the operations manager view the department as seen from a project manager's perspective and show where project management tools and techniques can be used to improve areas within the operation.

Is This for Me?

At this point the manager might be asking, "Is this really for me?" and "Is it necessary?" and "Will it make a difference?" The answer is a question: If the managers are truly the ones making adjustments to stay on course within their department, do they have the skills, knowledge, and tools to make effective adjustments in controlling resource management, budget control, process improvement, communication, training, risk management, and departmental organization? These are just some of the areas that will be covered in this book where project management tools and techniques have proven over and over to be very effective in operations management.

These tools and techniques do not require high levels of education, years of experience, or mathematical expertise—just that they are understood, implemented, and refined, given the manager's level of responsibility. For those who have been in management for several years, some of these techniques might seem familiar, but viewing them from a different perspective allows the tool to be sharpened and used in a better way. There might be some ideas that will generate some intrigue into how they can be used, or new items that might prove to be surprisingly effective.

Some managers might have been promoted to their position coming up through the ranks, and might be struggling with certain areas of how to manage or might not be familiar with areas of operation and could use more efficient tools to better control areas within the department. This can also be an opportunity to view the department from a different perspective and implement tools and techniques that can be very effective in changing how the department is monitored and controlled.

New managers or students of management can start their careers with a very cutting-edge and tactical approach in their management style that will prove to make them much more successful in not only managing but controlling a department. This perspective allows the manager to see other areas of the department more from a process standpoint and implement tools and techniques to effectively manage areas that other managers might be struggling with.

Senior and executive-level management can use these tools and techniques in training middle and lower-level management to improve their knowledge and skills in managing their responsibilities. It is frustrating to watch managers who report to you struggle in their approach to manage and control their department. The tools shown in this book will help managers see their department from a different perspective, allowing them to design monitoring systems and use control techniques to make adjustments that will streamline the operation. Improvements in overhead, processes, resource allocation, risk mitigation and elimination, communication, and waste management are some of the typical improvements that can be made using these tools.

Managers at all levels want to be successful and want to know that they are doing everything they can to manage all aspects within their responsibility. Having these tools and techniques in the manager's toolbox sets the manager apart as one who not only reports the outcome of what their department is doing, but can actually control and manage by making calculated adjustments that keep the department streamlined, cost-effective, and on course in completing its objective.

1

The Power of Completion

How Do You Gain Power from Completion?

Power in an organization can be defined in several ways, but this chapter focuses on the area of task and project completion and the types of power that can be accomplished through completion. Understanding power should not have us confined to the area of referent or authoritative power, but should challenge us to expand our critical thinking to explore where power can be found throughout a manager's leadership. Within management, there are areas over which managers have power or feel that they have more control, which can come across as power, and other areas that seem to be a power drain. Power can also be found in some of the most insignificant areas of leadership and might simply be overlooked or not even considered at all. The point is not in the mastery of control or gaining power; real power in management is accomplishment and completion. There is power great and small within leadership, and studying the area of completion will reveal tools that can be used to gain power in management and better develop your leadership skills.

Believing in the Task or Project

As a manager, you should recognize that your success in leadership with regard to managing tasks depends largely on two things: whether you believe in what you are doing and whether those who report to you believe in what you are doing. You have to be convinced that what you are undertaking is necessary if you want to be convincing to those who report to you. If you are not sold on the *idea* of the task, it will show in how you organize and manage the task. If you are excited about doing something, it will show in your organization or development of that task or project. You will be motivated to outline the steps that will be most efficient in completing the task because you recognize the value and really *want* it to be completed. You will put energy and time into planning and will choose the best resources to accomplish the task. You will schedule meetings to go over all the details to make sure everyone understands what is needed. Your level of detail and organization clearly shows everyone how much you believe in what you are doing. This carries over in not only displaying traits of your leadership but also communicating the importance of this task within the organization.

Those on the team will see that you believe in the task, and if it is important to you, it will be important to them. They will derive their loyalty to the project based on what they see in your leadership. They generally look to you as an example, so you need to ask yourself some important questions concerning your mind-set in overseeing a task or project:

1. Do you believe it is doable?
2. Do you believe that the human resources are competent enough to complete it?
3. Do you believe that the organization really needs this done and will benefit from it?

Power Tool

Power comes through a belief system that what you are doing means something—that you believe in it and support it. You will gain much more power in completing things *if you believe in what you are setting out to accomplish,* which will also *drive those who report to you to believe in the task* or project as well, giving you power to complete the task or project.

Proper Assessment of a Task or Project

The assessment starts the minute you are aware that something needs to be accomplished. The best project team in the company will not be able to complete a task if information about the task or project is missing or incorrect. To develop an accurate task or project plan, two areas need to be well defined and clearly understood:

1. **The scope**—Boundaries as to *only* what *needs* to be accomplished.

2. **The goal or deliverable**—What is the product, service, or desired output the task or project is assigned to produce.

In some cases the goal might be defined, but not understanding the boundaries or scope allows for tasks to expand or migrate beyond what was originally intended, making it harder or making it take longer to complete. Without a clearly defined scope, resources can get misdirected or distracted, leading them down a path that is unnecessary, wasting time and effort.

Power Tool

The power tool here involves helping the team *stay focused* on *only* what is required to ensure that they are efficient in completing their task.

Part of why completion might be difficult is that unrealistic goals might be set. If an overly optimistic completion time was set in a management meeting, a task can fail if that time frame is not attainable. If all the components of a task or project were not originally accounted for, an unrealistic time frame might have been set. In understanding the time requirements of task items, the manager must know how that information was obtained. Were the time frames simply your best guess or did you seek expert advice in getting accurate time assessments? One of the biggest problems with managing a task or project is holding to the schedule. If the schedule was built with inaccurate time information, holding to the schedule will be difficult, and you will feel you have no power in completing the task or project.

Power Tool

Accurate time frames and schedule information are necessary for developing the overall completion time that will be reported.

Having realistic time information will help match times during the execution of the task or project, ensuring that resources are more likely to stay on schedule. This is another way you build power in completing tasks.

Another area to consider is the skill set of the team. If the skill set of the team is inadequate to address the scope of the task, the task has a much higher probability of failure. Acquiring the appropriate skill sets within the team can have a very big impact on the success of the task. Some resources might overstate their abilities just to get on the team for notoriety. Other resources might be assigned to task teams by their manager even though they lack in their skill sets, but they might be the only resources available.

Power Tool

The ability of the manager to select or hire *staff with appropriate skill sets* is another way to build power in completing things in the organization.

Another part of proper assessment involves gathering information needed about the task or project. The power in completion actually goes back to the beginning, to having a clear scope of the goal and accurate cost and schedule data. Reporting on the status of a task might be accurate as to what is happening at that time but might appear over budget or behind schedule with reference to your original data set at the start of the task. If you had more accurate information at the beginning, reporting on the task will appear better if you are actually staying on course. So be careful about who is at fault here—if the team is doing their job, the numbers are only off because of inaccurate baseline data that you set at the beginning.

Managing a Task or Project

There is nothing more disappointing than being called into a meeting about a "new project" only to find that very little has been planned. The other disappointment is watching how disorganized the leader is, which will usually send a message to everyone about how the rest of the project is going to play out. This can also reveal that the manager does not believe in the task and has not invested time in planning it. Some managers pass this off as "I put the outline together and you guys run with it," which is just another way to communicate that you don't really support the task and you want the team to put it together and manage it.

Power Tool

Managers who believe in something will invest time in it and will *lead* it.

Organization is critical because the team is more likely to support the task or project if there appears to be time invested in organizing the task. Teams need leadership, direction, and organization; without these fundamental components there is no power in completion or, in most cases, any completion at all. Organizations that are not efficient can usually trace this back to a lack of leadership in their management that directly affects the bottom line. Most of what the working staff understands about the professionalism of the organization comes from their perception of management.

This can also trickle down to how staff members view the organization of task assignments and projects within the department. Do not underestimate the perception of a team because most teams can get a sense of buy-in and organization from the leader very quickly in the first meeting.

Power Tool

Being organized is good for both the manager and the team. Good organization involves *having specifics identified,* such as detailed tasks, names of people assigned to certain tasks and why, time frames and scopes of individual task items for those doing the tasks, and maybe even some potential risks.

Good organization is a sign that thought and time have been spent and care was taken to assess the details. The team will see this and realize how much this project means to the manager, which will drive the importance directly home to them. This is power in completing tasks or projects in your department. There has to be a driving force that steers the team, keeps them focused, assigns tasks, and holds them accountable to get things done. Teams that are left to develop the tasks on their own tend to struggle with arguments and run into delays, and team members become disinterested in the task because it doesn't appear to be important to anyone. These are the projects that fail. This doesn't mean that the manager always has to lead a team for them to be successful, but it means that there should be a designated leader and the entire team should know who is leading the team.

Accountability in Completing a Task or Project

Managing accountability requires two primary elements:

1. Having a clear understanding of what needs to be done

2. Being expected to produce the assigned task within a given time frame

Accountability applies to managers overseeing an assigned objective and the staff assigned the actual task items to be completed. The focus here is on having team players take ownership of task items and having the overseeing manager be held accountable for the task's completion. As just a reminder, managers are responsible for getting processes completed in their department and hiring staff to carry out the tasks. Team members need to be held to a quality standard in producing their task. It is one thing to complete an assignment, but the accountability needs to ensure completeness in both scope and quality of what is being produced.

Managers have a tendency to overcommit in meetings or to say that they will complete projects or task items when they don't really have the data to support what their team can actually do. This can be dangerous for the team because they had no input on the commitment but are now held accountable for that commitment. This can also be bad for the manager because it will be difficult to keep the team focused on the scope of the project and on schedule. Do not sell your team short by inaccurately committing, but rather find the correct information and then update the other managers on what you are committing to. This will increase your credibility with not only your peers but also your team.

Power Tool

Another tool in the power of completion and accountability is having *accurate data*. Try not to guess!

After the project is underway, the flow of information is critical. How often does the management team meet to get the status on tasks or projects? Meeting too often does not allow enough time for task items to complete, but not meeting frequently enough takes the accountability away from the managers in reporting accurately. Status meeting must be scheduled frequently enough to capture the right amount of data to be reported yet be efficient in management's time and mitigating of problems. Not knowing about problems as quickly as possible can have a detrimental effect on the task or project.

Take the Blinders Off

Managers are in a place of responsibility that requires thought and decision processing and when put to the test will reveal how well their decision process actually works. One of the process inhibitors that managers might encounter is working with paradigms. Managers might sometimes start down a path with a great idea of how they want to complete something, which is usually good but can have its drawbacks. Managers might operate in a rut, using the same old ways day in and day out, but not be pleased with the overall outcome of their department. Managers need to constantly look for improvements, and surprisingly they might find ideas in their department staff or management meetings. One of the power tools within an organization is team meetings, which, when conducted well, can produce several ideas and narrow them down to the best course of action. When a manager goes through the decision process, he should take a similar approach and evaluate other options because there might be more than one way to get something done.

Power Tool

Think out of the box and consider other alternatives.

Sticking to an original plan can be good, but consider being open-minded and looking into other ways to accomplish a task.

Power Tool

There might be others in the organization who have done something similar in the past whom you can consult to find out about *"lessons learned"* and mistakes that were made that you can avoid.

In some cases, brainstorming sessions with your team can reveal slightly different approaches that might be more efficient.

Power Tool

Brainstorming can touch on some team skills such as listening versus hearing and *information gathering meetings* that can reveal other ways to accomplish things.

These types of activities can be great for both discovering new things about your project and building a great team.

For the manager, this can be an eye-opening experience, revealing how many different alternatives there can be to accomplishing a task or project. This type of process approach can be a very effective decision-processing tool for the manager, as well as an opportunity to learn more about your team members and how the team interacts. This can also be used as an instructional tool for team building.

Power Tool

It is important for a manager to *keep an open mind* in how she approaches decision processing and to consider other areas for information that can help develop the best course of action.

Always keep this question in mind: "What is the fastest and most cost-effective way to complete a task or project correctly?"

Time Is of the Essence

Time is a vital resource within any organization. Many studies have been published that can quantify how much time companies waste each year and how much that can cost, not only in money but also in inefficient use of resources. One area that can be difficult to manage is human resource efficiency. It is a common fact that resources are not created equal and people will have both strengths and weaknesses. The manager hires human resources based largely on a skill set that shows strengths that can be used to perform required job functions. As these resources are in place to perform their required duty, they are sometimes called on to participate in other things such as additional tasks, projects, or team meetings. This can have one of two effects on a resource:

1. **Opportunity**—The resource is capable of performing the normal task and enjoys the opportunity to participate in other assignments, further developing the resource and improving his job satisfaction. *"They enjoy it."*

2. **Punishment**—The resource wants only to perform his required duty and feels that he should not have to be involved in other tasks or projects. This resource might or might not be capable of performing extra tasks and will see this as an increased stressful work environment. *"They hate it."*

In most cases a manager will present these opportunities by asking for volunteers, to get those most likely to embrace the opportunity and not see it as drudgery. The warning here is to not forget that this resource not only is performing her regular duty, but is taking on extra work and will need to have guidance in modifying her work schedule to include additional tasks. This is where problems can start and managers can either gain power or lose it.

Managers might come out of a meeting with an action item list and start throwing resources on new tasks just to get things started. Managers engaged in these new tasks or projects can get overly focused on completing those tasks and forget that these resources have their regular job to perform. Managers still have an operation to run and need to schedule these resources according to what the operation can afford. When these resources are off of their normal job, the organization suffers as a result. This is offset by what the resource is contributing on the special task that will benefit the organization. So as a net result the resource's time and completion of assignments is in balance relative to the bigger picture in the organization.

Power Tool

You have to *maintain a balance* of normal departmental duty work and special project work to make the most efficient use of resource time and benefit to the organization.

If too much time is spent on the special tasks, morale might decline because people get their satisfaction from performing their normal job.

There is a threshold that people will have in the balance of their normal job versus time spent on a special task that yields a certain job satisfaction. With some, too much time on the task takes them away from their normal job and they cross over the threshold and begin to resent the task for taking them away from their job, resulting in lower job satisfaction. On the other hand, there are people who thrive on the special task assignments and want to get away from their normal job to get the satisfaction they desire. They want to be on several tasks and avoid their normal job as much as possible. This might or might not be good for the organization or the resource. This topic is covered in Chapter 5, "Managing Your Resources."

Organizing a Task or Project

In talking with people in management, some of the most difficult things to accomplish are surprisingly not the big projects, but in many cases the smaller tasks. When you come out of management meetings, the larger projects usually have lots of resources, energy, focus, and managerial visibility associated with them. Larger projects typically are split into smaller subtasks that have individual work assignments associated with them. With so much focus on the large tasks, it is actually easier to get momentum going and for completion to be realized (lots of power). With the smaller tasks or projects there is less discussion about them in the initial meetings, few people are assigned to the project, and there is almost no focus or energy associated with them. They are not subdivided into smaller components, and getting traction and momentum going is difficult, leaving completion far from easy if it's even realized at all (no power).

Power Tool

When you have a task or project assignment, it is best to *break it up into smaller subtasks* that will allow for better definition of what is required and better management of each part.

One of the problems with initially structuring a project relates to going into enough detail on the tasks to cover *all* the items that will need to be completed. If this data is not accurate, the manager is starting off with incomplete information about the project that can result in inaccurate schedule or cost information. There are several benefits to breaking down tasks or projects into smaller parts:

- Creates an outline form of the task or product to better view all work required.
- Breaks up the project into major components or steps.
- Makes it easier to define each step and breaks steps into smaller work packages.

- Reduces the chance of forgetting required steps.
- Makes it easier to communicate the work to the project team.
- Creates a better resource scheduling tool.
- Enables the project to run more efficiently.
- Allows the manager to have better problem and risk management.
- Enables the manager to more accurately report the status.

When projects are broken up into smaller components, resources are likely to view their part as a smaller, easier task to complete than if they see their part listed as a single large item taking a long time to complete. Part of the power in this tool stems from *the perception the resource has of his work.* This can be a perception of his regular duty or of an additional task he volunteered for. In many cases the title of Manager or Director can be daunting due to the responsibility involved, but in reality it is just a bunch of smaller jobs that make up that title. How a resource views what he is required to do can play a big role in his perception of a workload. Breaking up projects or tasks into smaller parts allows the resource to see that it might be much easier to complete a large item than originally thought. This can be equally beneficial for the manager. This is also how project managers view a project and how they communicate the tasks, as just small parts that each resource needs to focus on.

Managers are more successful when they have a sense of organization and control over tasks being worked on in their department. Managers should look for ways to make their department run more efficiently and should have more details on what resources are doing, allowing the manager more information to consider alternatives. When managers have the ability to actually manage and control the work performed in their department, they feel better about their job. People working on a project or working in that department can see that the manager is organized, has a sense of vision and direction as to the work being performed, and knows what the end goal is leading up to.

This also promotes accountability within the department or team as resources can see more details about what is required and when.

Power Tool

The power of completion is in *organization* that allows *more control over the work being performed.* This is seen not just in reporting on tasks, but also in actually feeling as though you have control over your resources, task detail, and scheduling options as a result of better task organization.

One tool used in project management that the operations manager can use to better organize a department is a work breakdown structure, or WBS, as shown in Table 1.1.

This structure can be built using Microsoft Excel or Microsoft Project. The work breakdown structure is used to subdivide work into smaller tasks. You can continue to break down these subtasks as far as you need to go until you get to what's called the work package. This helps the manager organize tasks in sequence and reveals which subtasks need to be completed before others can start, which is called the predecessor. Predecessors help the manager understand the flow of work and sequence of tasks. This also helps the manager understand, from an accountability standpoint, who will need to complete their work before other work can start.

The manager can also use this work breakdown structure to assign resources to tasks, smaller subtasks, and work packages. The manager can use these resource assignments for those overseeing a task or the people actually doing the task. Other things can be assigned in the work breakdown structure, such as costs for resources and materials, start and stop times that define the timeframe in which a task will need to be completed, and quality checkpoints. This tool can be used for projects or general organization of a department that has several components of work that need to be scheduled in sequence.

Table 1.1 Work Breakdown Structure Illustrated in Microsoft Excel

Task	WBS Code	Project Tasks	Durations	Predecessor	Resources
1	1	**Project Name**	**33 Days Total**		
2	1.1	**First Subtask**	**14 Days Subtotal**		
3	1.1.1	Lower Divided Subtask or Work Package	2 Days		Name
4	1.1.2	Lower Divided Subtask or Work Package	7 Days		Name
5	1.1.2.1	Lowest-Level Work Package	4 Days	3	Name
6	1.1.2.2	Lowest-Level Work Package		5	Name
7	1.1.3	Lower Divided Subtask or Work Package	5 Days	6	Name
8	1.2	**Second Subtask**	**8 Days Subtotal**		
9	1.2.1	Lower Divided Subtask or Work Package	5 Days	7	Name
10	1.2.2	Lower Divided Subtask or Work Package	3 Days	9	Name
11	1.3	**Third Subtask**	**11 Days Subtotal**		
12	1.3.1	Lower Divided Subtask or Work Package	7 Days	10	Name
13	1.3.2	Lower Divided Subtask or Work Package	4 Days	12	Name

The work breakdown structure can help the manager not only see information relative to tasks and resources, but also better organize and plan for resources that will be used later on the project. The manager might also want to use a WBS to help capture all the tasks that need to be done on a large project. When large projects are first organized, it can be difficult to understand everything that needs to be completed because there might be a large amount of work to be done or it might span a long duration of time. Starting off with main subdivided parts of the project can act as an information repository that can be further organized to define the work that needs to be completed. In most cases further refinement is in allocation of resources.

One area of concern in operations management is resource management. Resources can be in the form of facilities, capital equipment, cash or lines of credit, IT and communications systems, and human resources. In the work breakdown structure, the manager can assign not only human resources to tasks, but also other resources that might be required to complete a project. This is critical for efficiency within the organization because most companies do not have an unlimited supply of resources and an organized scheduling structure. Some resources needed by a manager might be critical, such as a line of credit, expensive equipment, corporate aircraft, or resources used by an outside company or contractor. These types of resources require special care and in some cases require contracts to be written that will define the scope of what is needed by the resource. Financial resources can be small and easily managed within the department or they can be very large, requiring a line of credit or a significant amount of the company's financial resources. This is when the manager could use a work breakdown structure to help other managers like financial managers understand when critical pieces of finances need to be used on a project.

One thing midlevel managers might not be aware of is the amount of cash flow required by a company. Cash flow is typically used for such things as salaries, materials, equipment, and running the operation, but when a special task or project is underway, extra financial resources might be required to complete critical things on a project or areas of the operation. Using a WBS works well with coordinating tasks on a project or cost-sensitive areas of the operation with the financial department to not only plan cash flow but also coordinate with all the departments in the organization. This is done differently at various levels of management and responsibility.

If the manager has responsibility over a single department, overseeing special projects within that department might be more simplified. In this case, the manager is generally more focused on the people and details of tasks being done. Another level might be the operations manager in charge of several departments or facilities. This level of management requires a more organizational approach and tools like a work breakdown structure to help with identification and the sequence of processes or defining of special projects. It will be important to coordinate resources used on normal departmental activities and those on special projects. This type of tool brings organization, definition, logistics, resources, and accountability all together and makes them all visible in one single tool and increases your power as a manager in completing tasks.

Should a Task Become an Official Project?

Much of what will be discussed involves the organization of a department and/or special projects. Because most departments have normal day-to-day tasks they carry out, one critical management step is in determining when a normal task performed in the department should be treated like a project. Project tasks will appear to have a start and stop and be unique from the other things in the department. They can be special things like process or documentation development, facilities or organizational things, or training to help improve the department or staff. If something is a repetitive task, it is generally not a project. If something will be done once or is set apart from the normal tasks in the department, it might be a project. In some cases a unique task "project" will be big enough to have a project manager (which might be you). These are tasks big enough to be broken up into resource teams and be organized in big project-type steps. In any case, the manager needs to assess tasks and processes in the department to determine whether they are normal operations tasks or projects. This is a critical step in completing tasks as the manager needs to determine projects versus normal everyday processes.

Operations Manager or Project Manager—Who Are You?

The status meeting is the test of the operations manager to see whether she can really manage a task or project. In most cases the manager is good at managing the department, but when special tasks are assigned, how does the manager perform then? One of the first setbacks that you as a manager will have to deal with is not being able to complete a task and coming back to the next status meeting to report that you need more time. This might be acceptable once, but the next time this happens the team will start to lose confidence in your leadership ability. Another problem with this is that the more you get used to pushing dates out, the easier it will be to keep pushing them out, and you then are no longer in a task completion mode but a task maintenance mode (reactive). This task has then become a regularly scheduled event; the team has realized that you no longer believe in the task and it has fallen in importance.

Executive management is looking at not only the ability of managers to accomplish their normal responsibilities, but also how successful they are at running special tasks and projects and getting them done! This is primarily the ability to *complete* special tasks or projects. When scheduled completion dates are accurately assessed and hit on a project, the manager knows that the team did a good job when completing the task. This doesn't mean that the manager can just push out the dates to ensure that they will always be met, because then these tasks would drag on too long. Managers have to be diligent in sticking to the schedule and managing teams to get things done. In some cases it might be wise to get more accurate information about completion dates instead of committing to a schedule knowing that it's not realistic.

This can be the first step in understanding how to gain power in completion. Try to improve your process of being better organized as a manager, taking a few extra steps in understanding what you are getting yourself and your team into. Most mistakes made can usually be tracked back to *poor assessment* of time, resources, or cost or scope of the task, and this results in tasks either not getting completed or taking too long to complete. This is when the operations manager is not thinking like a project manager and is focusing too much attention on the department's normal work and not enough time on special tasks that need a detailed mind like that of a project manager. The operations manager can do this; they just need to know when and have some basic tools to help organize the project. Completing these special projects on time and efficiently saves the organization time and money, increasing power in both the manager and the organization. The other way to view this is in the organization of normal everyday processes and how much control or power the manager has in accomplishing those tasks.

Managing Processes Versus Reporting on Progress

Most managers are in a position to oversee tasks or processes being completed, but managers are not always sure how to fix something if a task goes wrong or is not being completed the way it is supposed to be done. As processes are being completed, problems or setbacks will come up that can cause delays in the schedule. In most cases the manager reports delays or problems in something like a manager's meeting or status meeting. What the manager is really communicating is their "observation" of the problem and not the steps showing how they are "managing" the fix.

One key part of effective managing is the manipulation of resources to improve processes or a project budget and/or schedule. There are two fundamental approaches in overseeing processes or projects: *reporting* and *managing*. In reporting, the manager is *observing* the team progress and reporting the status. In managing, there is the *manipulation* of things within the project that allows the manager to bring a project back on schedule or budget. This is accomplished first by outlining all the tasks that need to be completed and setting a baseline of project cost and schedule. As a project progresses, you can compare real-time data to the baseline to monitor any deviations and look for ways to shift resources to get costs or the schedule back in line. Depending on how you have your task or project set up, there are some tools that can help bring things back on schedule, several of which are covered in later chapters.

When a process is being completed, resources need to know what to do if something goes wrong. The manager can add more resources to improve the schedule, or in other cases the manager can purchase or lease something that will help fix the problem. In any case, the manager needs to have some idea as to how to fix a problem, and this goes into the area of risk assessment, management, and being able to actually identify potential problems before they happen.

Power Tool

Assessing areas of risk is not hard; it just requires some time spent asking questions of key individuals about what can go wrong so that you can plan for the problems.

Planning for problems is a great way to "manage" a process or project because you feel you have more control when you have tried to account for details such as potential risks.

Power Tools for the Manager

Here's how to get back on track:

1. **Doing tasks simultaneously**—If there are several tasks in a row, each having to be completed before the next can start, then reevaluate the sequence to see whether that is necessary. There might be a couple of tasks that can be run together or in parallel, allowing you to get you back on schedule.

2. **Sequencing of task starts and stops**—In the initial layout of a project, you have certain tasks that have to be completed before the next task can start. Reevaluate whether that is true because there might be other tasks that can start before all the requirements of the previous task have been completed. This will allow you to get a jump on the schedule.

3. **Adding more resources from other tasks**—You might have to get more resources for a given task or process that is taking too long to complete. Remember, resources can be anything the organization has, whether human, equipment, computers, or lines of credit. Temporarily adding a few more human resources on a task can bring it back on schedule and help the overall completion date. Every day you slip adds to the end date!

4. **Evaluating the scope or requirement of the task**—What did you set out to accomplish and did you bite off more than you could chew? Sometimes taking another look at what you are doing can help bring focus back to the team. Teams also have a tendency to get distracted and drift off topic, putting them behind. Keep the team focused on the task at hand.

5. **Determining whether you have the right skill sets on this project or task**—Evaluate who is on your team or in the department and whether they really have the skills to complete the tasks and processes on schedule and on budget. It is great to

have lesser-skilled resources on a task to give them the experience they need in order to improve. There is a schedule and a budget that also have to be met, however, and if those resources will likely struggle to hit those targets, you might have to get them a little help or consider another, more skilled resource.

The manager might be overseeing several tasks and processes and might need to act as a program or project manager. This requires some other skills or knowledge that managers might not have. Depending on how high up the managers are and how many departments they oversee, they might view their departments like projects within a program to help organize them. How do you view your organization—as a department with a bunch of resources doing stuff? Or do you view it as a bunch of smaller groups or cells like small project groups?

One rule in organizing operations is to break things down into smaller components. This allows you to visualize and see the separate parts of your organizations more clearly. This is why a CEO doesn't manage all the departments in the organization, because they would just see one mass of resources. When an organization is broken down into smaller departments, the CEO can see separate functional parts of the company being managed independently.

The operations manager needs to view his department or organization the same way, as smaller groups or components, to better monitor and control his department. This is also taken down another level to completing tasks, processes, or projects as you break them down into smaller pieces to better understand the goal of the task and help organize the resources working on the task. Depending on how big the process or project is, you might have to break down each piece further into smaller subtasks.

Organization starts with the "view" or perception managers have of what they are managing. One of the successful tools project managers have is the visibility of the project, and breaking the project down gives better clarity of the details. Viewing the department in smaller pieces helps give clarity and detail to what is being done, allowing the manager to actually "manage" tasks, costs, and schedules so that completion is realized. This also allows the manager to take on special projects as well and see them to completion, giving the manager power in what they are trying to accomplish. The perception will be of organization, visibility, and knowing that they are more in *control* than simply watching. Managers need to know that they have the ability to make changes if needed, and using key tools will give the manager confidence to *"manage."*

Power Tool Summary

- Power comes through a belief system that what you are doing means something—that you believe in it and support it. You will gain much more power completing things *if you believe in what you are setting out to accomplish,* which will also *drive those who report to you to believe in the task* or project as well, giving you power to complete the task or project.

- The power tool here involves helping the team *stay focused* on *only* what is required to ensure that they are efficient in completing their task.

- Accurate time frames and schedule information are necessary for developing the overall completion time that will be reported. Having realistic time information will help match times during the execution of the task or project, ensuring that resources are more likely to stay on schedule. This is another way you build power in completing tasks.

- The ability of the manager to select *staff with appropriate skill sets* is another way to build power in completing things in the organization.

- Managers who believe in something will invest time in it and will *lead* it.

- *Being organized is good for both the manager and the team.* Good organization involves *having specifics identified,* such as detailed tasks, names of people assigned to certain tasks and why, time frames and scopes of individual task items for those doing the tasks, and maybe even some potential risks.

- Another tool in the power of completion and in accountability is having *accurate data.* Try not to guess!

- *Think out of the box* and consider other alternatives.

- There might be others in the organization who have done something similar in the past whom you can consult to find out *"lessons learned"* and mistakes that were made that you can avoid.

- Brainstorming can touch on some team skills such as listening versus hearing and *information gathering meetings* that can reveal other ways to accomplish things.

- It is important for a manager to *keep an open mind* in how she approaches decision processing and to consider other areas for information that can help develop the best course of action.

- You have to *maintain a balance* of normal departmental duty work and special project work to make the most efficient use of resource time and benefit to the organization.

- When you have a task or project assignment, it is best to *break it up into smaller subtasks* that will allow for better definition of what is required and better management of each part.

- The power of completion is in *organization that allows more control over work being performed.* This is seen not just in reporting on tasks, but also in actually feeling as though you have control over your resources, task detail, and scheduling options as a result of better task organization.

- *Assessing areas of risk* is not hard; it just requires some time spent asking questions of key individuals about what can go wrong so that you can plan for the problems.

  Planning for problems is a great way to "manage" a process or project because you feel you have more control when you have tried to account for details such as potential risks.

2

Communication Is King

If we were to survey executive and midlevel management about what they feel were the most important elements of success, effective communication would probably rank in at least the top five. Organizations do not operate in a vacuum where no communication is required either internally or externally. If there are at least two people in an organization and this organization has to connect in some way with the outside world, communication will play a big role in their success. If this component within the organization is so important, it must be understood, developed, and implemented like any other process.

If communication can be developed as a process, one must understand what the deliverable or outcome of this process should be, and then work back through the process to develop steps to accomplish that deliverable. This might generate some interesting discussion as to what the deliverable would actually be! One might say *effective* communication, while another might say *quality* communication or *timely and accurate* communication. Because these are great goals in developing a communication plan, it must be understood *what is being communicated,* to *whom,* and *why,* and let that point to defining the deliverable of the communication process.

Although communication can happen in several different formats, such as human to human, human to machine, and machine to machine, this chapter focuses on human-to-human interaction. The fundamental goal in communication is one human trying to convey a thought, idea, command, or piece of information to another human being. Although this sounds simple, there are several things happening in the communication process that can play a role in the success of communication.

Why Communication?

Communication is required at all levels within the organization: between employees at the task level, managers to workers, management to management, executive management to mid-level and lower-level management, as well as business to business. All of these groups represent a wide variety of backgrounds, educational and intellectual, as well as different cultural, professional, and social levels. This represents the first complexity that must be considered in developing a communication process. The organization might have established processes and policies concerning the appropriate communication within the organization, and this should be reviewed when a communication process is being developed.

The next component of communication is the general formal or informal nature of communication. It is important for management to know when it is appropriate to use formal versus informal types of communication. Formal communication is typically used more in contractual agreements, bids and proposals, legal documentation, and other forms of business-to-business information transfer. Informal communication might be more in the form of internal memos, status meetings, and one-on-one conversations to convey information. In either case there is always a sender and a receiver of information, and all of the above considerations will play a factor in designing an effective communications plan.

The Communication Path

To better understand communication, you must first look at what is happening in the communication process that allows information to be transferred from one human to another. At this point one would say that this starts with the formation of words leaving one person's mouth and another person hearing those words. Although that is true, fundamentally, you have to understand that the *process* of communicating is *effectively conveying a piece of information from one human to another*. Communication can take the form of audible words, hand motions, body language, or written words that can be interpreted through sight or touch. Because the scope of this chapter is more the development of communication tools, it is important to understand what communicating actually is without going into great detail.

The fundamental goal of communication is to make a connection between the sender and the receiver. This forms a path that both the sender and the receiver will play an important role in developing and maintaining. Let's look briefly at some important aspects of both sending and receiving information.

Sender

The sender is the person who has information they need to convey to another person or a group of people. It is important that the sender be clear and concise about the information they want to convey. One common problem with senders is the balance between conveying too much information and conveying not enough information, each potentially coming across as confusing. This will put the receiver at a disadvantage because this information might be difficult to decipher and might make it difficult for the receiver to draw the conclusion that the sender intended.

Senders must also take care that the format in which information is being conveyed does not cause problems in transmitting the information from one human to another. For example, if two people were talking on a construction site while heavy equipment was being operated, having a verbal conversation might be difficult because of the noise. This might result in the receiver's understanding only part of the information, in which case the message transfer was not successful. It is the responsibility of the sender to choose a form of communication that will *effectively transfer* the entire message the sender intended for the receiver.

The sender can choose a one-to-one conversation to better artic-ulate information and generate discussion between the sender and the receiver for further verification of facts within the information being transferred. The sender might choose a written form to best clarify the message if there is important detailed information to be conveyed. The written form might also be chosen due to distance or time zones, and e-mail might best convey a message in a timely and accurate manner. It is the sender's responsibility to choose the best form of communication transfer to completely and accurately convey information or a message.

Receiver

The receiver, the other half of the information transfer connec-tion, is as important as the sender. The receiver also has responsibili-ties in this connection to verify the information he has received and to make sure that he understands the message that was sent. If the receiver is having a verbal conversation with a sender, it's important that he makes and keeps a connection to ensure that everything the sender conveyed was received. The receiver in many cases will show signs of receiving information in the form of body language or confir-mation in statements, which confirm that he understands the message that was sent. The receiver's body language might indicate that he is not paying full attention if he is nervous, distracted, or disinterested in the conversation. This can also point to the difference between listening and hearing.

Listening Versus Hearing

There are two forms of reception the receiver will engage in: hearing and listening. Hearing is the physical ability to receive audible sounds in the human ear. Although the sender's words move through the air and strike the receiver's ears, this does not indicate that communication has happened. Hearing is simply sound waves striking the eardrum. It is the second component, that of listening, in which the receiver decodes those sound waves into an actual message. Receivers must understand that it is *listening* that will determine whether a message was conveyed. Listening is the receiver decoding information into a message that the sender intended the receiver to understand. How does the sender know whether the receiver understood a message? This is detected in what's called a feedback system.

Feedback

Feedback is the receiver sending a signal of some kind that indicates whether she received, and understood, all the information. It's vitally important in conversations between individuals, or for an individual within a group, that feedback is detected because this allows the sender to understand that receivers are actually listening to their message and not just hearing information bounce off their ears. Feedback can be displayed as body language, hand movements, or facial expressions in which receivers are sending a message that they do or do not understand information. It might be in the form of questions showing that they understand part of the information but need further clarification to understand the full message. This feedback can also be associated with other forms of communication, such as e-mail, telephone, and video conferencing, during which the sender should be watching for signs of feedback to ensure that communication is effective and their message has been received and understood. This connection between the sender and the receiver is vitally important because it is the foundation for effectively transferring information within the organization.

Communication Applications

One-to-One

Managers sometimes find themselves in situations in which it is appropriate to have one-to-one communication. This is typically in the form of a manager giving a worker performance reviews, disciplinary action, or maybe training or instruction at the individual level.

Power Tool

The manager, being the sender, must design the conversation with a *clear objective* and conduct the conversation *in a place appropriate to effectively convey the message* without distraction. It is also important for the manager to *pay attention to feedback* from the individual or to *solicit a response* to confirm that the information has been received and understood by the individual.

One-to-one communication can result in any number of outcomes. This can involve the manager's having a simple conversation conveying information that was understood by the individual with little or no reaction. Conversations can result in discussion going back and forth, clarifying information, or generating new ideas that take the conversation in a different direction. This can also result in arguments if the receiver did not like the information and the feedback communicated displeasure with the information. In any case one-to-one discussion allows for the clearest communication path and the clearest feedback and discussion opportunity.

One-to-Group

This form of communication requires one individual to convey a message to several individuals in one setting. This might be easier for some people than one-to-one; in other cases this might be perceived as more difficult depending on the skill and experience of the sender. This form of communication is typical within the organization when managers are broadcasting general information to those in their department, or when executive managers are broadcasting information to the entire organization. There might be those teaching at educational institutes who will use this form of communication in the classroom to teach a group of students. In some cases the organization might have a manager engaged in training a group of individuals for a particular process.

Although this is slightly different from one-to-one, there is still a path and connection made with each individual within the group. The information still has to go to each individual, it must be decoded and understood, and the same feedback mechanism must be established to understand that the individuals have received and understood the message. Receivers, in the group setting, might not verbally give feedback with questions but might indicate through body language whether they are attentive.

Power Tool

It is important for the *sender to pay attention to body language* because this might be the only indicator that messages were received and understood. It is also a good practice for the sender to solicit questions to clarify receivers' understanding.

One-to-Several Locations

Organizations in this day and age are extending their operations to multiple locations that might include other areas of the country and the world. This can add a level of complexity to the communication path but should not discourage the manager from developing a communication plan for off-site locations. Interestingly enough, even with off-site locations or locations around the world, the communication path still exists, with a sender, the form or path the information will travel, and a receiver, as well as a feedback system. As long as these components make up the communication process, communication can be accomplished anywhere, at any level, with any complexity of operations.

Note

When communicating to multiple locations, the manager needs to understand that the sender and message have not changed, nor have the receiver and listening function. *The only change is in the path or format chosen to deliver the information.*

This becomes the make-or-break point of multilocation communication in sending and receiving information accurately and completely. These paths can be in the form of e-mail, conference call, or teleconference. Much as in the individual and group setting, the sender should try to design a message that can be sent clearly and look for feedback which indicates that the message was received and understood.

When the manager understands that the components of communication are the same, simply taking different forms of transfer depending on the scenario, managers can treat the communication as a process developing and improving as needed.

Power Tool

It is when managers can see *many areas of operations as processes* that simply need to be developed and improved that they have *the tools to approach critical areas in operations confidently.*

Communicating in Meetings

It is common to find managers performing the communication function in a one-to-group or meeting format. Meetings are conducted as a place where information is transferred, and how these meetings are structured and conducted plays a large role in the success of the information being transferred. As you have seen, there is a communication path that will be established in transferring information, but potential difficulties can be compounded in a group setting where there are other dynamics to be considered.

Meetings, depending on the purpose, can have varying types of staff that might present other issues to consider. These issues might simply be personality conflicts, varying agendas, or various levels of management that might be represented with no particular reason. It is important for the manager to understand why meetings are conducted, what are they designed to accomplish, and who needs to attend. In conducting meetings, the manager can do certain things before, during, and after the meeting to ensure that information is successfully transferred and understood by those attending the meeting.

Before-Meeting Prep

Confirm that the meeting is necessary

Identify the participants

Establish an agenda

Prepare meeting logistics such as conference calls or computer links

During the Meeting

Start the meeting on time

Designate a meeting minutes taker

Facilitate the meeting, manage the agenda

Summarize the meeting results

Summarize follow-up actions

After the Meeting

Distribute meeting notes and list of follow-up actions

Plan for any follow-up meetings

The manager must also understand that every time there is a meeting, resources are stepping away from their normal job to participate in that meeting. It should also be understood that these meetings cost the organization time and money. This places the responsibility on the shoulders of the person calling for the meeting to justify everyone's need to participate. It is also important, depending on the topics of discussion and information that will be shared, to properly determine the participants who need access to that information. This is one factor in why some meetings go better than others and why some participants should or should not have been a part of the meeting. The manager should also consider the type of meeting being called, why it's being called, and who should participate in each type of meeting.

The following are some examples of various types of meetings that can be conducted within the organization:

- Department or staff meeting
- Project kickoff meeting
- Status review meeting
- Problem-solving meeting
- Design review meeting
- Customer, supplier, or vendor meeting

All of these types of meetings have certain things in common: They have a sender of information, a communication path, a receiver, and a feedback component. The manager in charge of setting up these meetings will have these components of communication to consider no matter how many people are involved, how many locations are involved, or the dynamics of the individuals involved. The process of communication is still the same—it simply takes different forms.

Power Tool

The manager thinking of communication as a process can design communication at any level or scenario required.

When the manager understands that *communication is a process,* she can formulate a communication plan that can act as a check-off list when communication is required.

Communication Management Plan

The communication management plan is a project management tool that establishes a checklist of how a project manager conducts communication within a project. This can also be used by the manager to set up meetings and establish communication protocol within the operation. To help improve the process of communication, managers must know more of the details and characteristics of the environment within the organization. The communication management plan is a simple matrix that lists four fundamental areas of communication: who, what, when, and how.

1. **Who**—In establishing meetings, who needs to be at the meeting is vitally important to the success of the meeting. When information is released, either announced by the manager or offered by others in the meeting, it is important for the manager to understand who really needs this information. As mentioned, all the resources invited to the meeting have been taken away from their primary duty in order to participate in this meeting. Although these individuals might have a need for the information in the meeting, they will need to return to their primary responsibility as quickly as possible.

   Care must be taken in deciding whether certain management and executive management need to attend, because a lower-level meeting with lots of detail might not require their participation. Other status meetings can be designed to update higher levels of management on larger components of the operation. Likewise, workforce individuals might be required in a meeting for their level of detail or status update, but might not be required in other meetings where higher levels of information or sensitive information will be distributed. It is important that the manager only invite necessary resources who either will participate in giving information or are needed to receive information in a particular meeting.

2. **What**—Information is a powerful tool within an organization, and managers must be responsible for what types of information are distributed through various levels within the organization. Executive managers typically do not want to sit in on low-level update or status meetings and listen to all the discussions and detail within that type of meeting. Likewise, workforce employees should not be attending executive management meetings where they would be privileged to sensitive information and decisions required at that level. So meetings are designed around specific information being distributed to certain individuals who require this information as part of their job.

Information can be given in several forms, from verbal status to PowerPoint-type slide presentations to detailed drawings. The point of the meeting is to accurately and completely convey information, so it is vital that the information be in the appropriate form and be as clear as possible. When using graphs and charts, make sure that the receiver understands what information is there and what is being said. It is in these settings that information is misunderstood, and the sender must make sure that the format does not cause problems. These meetings are designed specifically to match the information that is discussed with the participants who will be required to hear this information.

3. **When**—Now that the manager has established what type of meetings is needed, who will be invited to these meetings, and what information will be distributed and discussed, it's

important to determine whether meetings need to be held on an ongoing basis. Some meetings are held to distribute information in a single setting, whereas other meetings are set up on a regular or ongoing basis. As previously mentioned, because resources attending these meetings will be taken away from their normal responsibilities, meetings should be held only as often as needed. Meetings do cost the organization time and money so too many meetings are simply a waste! The frequency at which ongoing meetings are held needs to be evaluated by the manager to ensure that information is transferred in a timely manner, without requiring overly frequent meetings.

4. **How**—The last component in developing the communication management plan is to determine how information will be communicated. The manager needs to determine the appropriate communication path required for each type of information needing to be communicated, depending on to whom it needs to go and where these individuals will be. Because information can be delivered in several forms, it is important that the manager understand that the type of communication selected should match the type of information that needs to be transferred. For example, a short statement about a change or status can be simply e-mailed, whereas a discussion about a change requiring a decision might constitute a meeting to facilitate that discussion. Details about a drawing might be best communicated if the receivers can see the details for themselves on the drawing rather than reading them in a typed paragraph within an e-mail or hearing them in a discussion on the phone. The form of communication is very important for the manager to choose in transferring information because this can dictate the success of understanding what was intended in the message.

Some managers and executives are more comfortable with e-mails and conference calls and simply would prefer that form of communication. Others might prefer being in meetings for the discussion and want an e-mail summary after the meeting. The manager needs to know how others prefer receiving information because this might also dictate how comfortable the receiver is while trying to understanding a message, or it might be that they are very busy and simply cannot attend every meeting.

A simple tool used in project management to consolidate the details of who, what, when, and how information will be distributed is called a communication matrix. This is another tool the manager can develop. It can start with four columns listing the preceding items and all those within the department and organization with whom the manager will communicate listed in the rows. Tables 2.1 and 2.2 show examples of how a communication matrix can be used in operations management. These can be listed by either meeting or resource type.

This tool is useful because the manager can quickly see which individuals are supposed to attend which type of meetings, how often the meetings are scheduled, and what type of communication these individuals prefer. It is also important for the manager to discuss with each individual his preferred form of communication because this might help in the communication path. Some individuals who attend a meeting might also ask for a follow-up e-mail of the minutes and actions assigned. Other individuals might not elect to attend the meeting but might prefer an e-mail containing the minutes because of their time constraints and other responsibilities. Some resources could be located in other facilities or around the world and might request a conference call or videoconference as well as an e-mail. It is the responsibility of the manager to determine how these individuals are to participate and what their preferred form of communication is in order to ensure the success of communication.

Table 2.1 Communication Matrix Example—By Meeting Type

Meeting Type	Owner	Frequency	Recipients	Delivery Medium	Deliverable
Department Gen Communications	Operations Manager	Bimonthly	All Dept Staff	Face to Face	Announcements
			Dept Supervisors	Face to Face/E-mail	Topic Discussions
Department Supervisor Update	Operations Manager	Weekly	Dept Supervisors	Face to Face/E-mail	Meeting Minutes
Management Status	VP of Operations	Weekly	Operations Mgr	Face to Face/E-mail	Meeting Minutes
			Facilities, Acct Mgrs	Face to Face/E-mail	
			Engineering Mgr	Conf Call/E-mail	
Documentation Review	Document Control Mgr	Monthly	Operations Mgr	Face to Face/E-mail	Meeting Minutes
			Engineering Mgr	Face to Face/E-mail	Docs for Review
Safety Committee	Committee Chairman	Monthly	Operations Mgr	Face to Face/E-mail	Meeting Minutes
			Facilities Mgr	Face to Face/E-mail	Action List
			Engineering Mgr	Conf Call/E-mail	
Special Project Status Review	Project Manager	As Needed	Operations Mgr	Face to Face/E-mail	Meeting Minutes
			Engineering Mgr	Conf Call/E-mail	Action List
			Project Logistics	Conf Call/E-mail	

Table 2.2 Communication Matrix Example—By Resource Type

Resource Type	Meetings to Attend	Frequency	Preferred Delivery	Correspondence
VP of Division	Management Status	Weekly	Face to Face/Email	Meeting Minutes
Facilities Mgr	Management Status	Weekly	Face to Face/E-mail	Meeting Minutes
	Safety Committee	Monthly	Face to Face/E-mail	Meeting Minutes/Action List
Engineering Mgr	Management Status	Weekly	Conf Call/E-mail	Meeting Minutes
	Documentation Review	Monthly	Face to Face/E-mail	Meeting Minutes/Docs for Review
	Safety Committee	Monthly	Conf Call/E-mail	Meeting Minutes/Action List
	Project Status Review	As Needed	Conf Call/E-mail	Meeting Minutes/Action List
Project Mgr	Project Status Review	As Needed	Face to Face/E-mail	Meeting Minutes/Action List
HR & Accounting Mgr	Management Status	Weekly	Face to Face/E-mail	Meeting Minutes
Dept Supervisors	Dept General Communications	Bimonthly	Face to Face	Announcements/Topic Discussions
	Dept Supervisor Update	Weekly	Face to Face/E-mail	Meeting Minutes/Action List

When the manager develops the communication management plan and understands the communication path as a process, this becomes a powerful tool for the manager to better refine how information is transferred within the organization. The simple knowledge of the communication path and developing a tool like a communication matrix helps the manager work with other individuals in delivering information as they prefer. When recipients of information receive only the information they need, when they need it, and in the form that is preferred by them, this increases the success of how information is used and processed within the operation.

Power Tool

The manager has *more power* over completing tasks and control over information distribution, giving the manager's *confidence* and *improving* the communication structure within the organization.

Power Tool Summary

- The manager, being the sender, must design the conversation with a *clear objective* and conduct the conversation *in a place appropriate to effectively convey the message* without distraction. It also is important for the manager to *pay attention to feedback* from the individual or to *solicit a response* to confirm that the information has been received and understood by the individual.

- It is important for the *sender to pay attention to body language* because this might be the only indicator that messages were received and understood. It is also good practice for the sender to solicit questions to clarify receivers' understanding.

- It is when managers can see *many areas of operations as processes* that simply need to be developed and improved that they have *the tools to approach critical areas in operations confidently*.
- The manager thinking of communication as a process can design communication at any level or scenario required.
- The manager has *more power* over completing tasks and control over information distribution, giving the manager's *confidence* and *improving* the communication structure within the organization.

3

Fix the Processes

What Is a Process?

In an ever-changing world one thing remains constant: Organizations are established to produce a product, service, or desired output of some kind. Organizations can be in the form of a service, distribution, design and manufacturing of products, consulting, nonprofit, or government institutions. In any case, resources are at work doing something. As an organization matures, it develops a systematic flow of tasks that will accomplish this desired output. Each task becomes a specific element of work or set of work elements that when completed accomplish the task. The systematic organization of these work elements are referred to as a process. Processes should be one of the most important components of an organization because they are intended to define how the organization performs tasks.

Power Tool

Defined processes should be found all throughout the organization and should be documented to record and communicate how series of tasks are designed and sequenced to complete a process.

Large amounts of time and effort can go into developing good processes, but if they are not documented and effectively communicated, there can still be problems with the quality and accuracy of completed tasks. Problems in an organization such as poor quality, damaged materials, rework, slower than expected performance, and poor on-time delivery can be linked back to three fundamental areas:

1. No documented processes

2. Incorrectly documented processes

3. Processes documented well but not performed correctly

Problems occurring from a lack of documented processes leave the door open to incorrect interpretation of how things are to be done. This can promote "tribal knowledge," or the verbal passing down of task information, which increases the risk of incomplete or inaccurate information and poor task performance. A lack of monitoring can lead to not knowing why processes are performed incorrectly. In many cases managers struggle with processes and wonder why things just aren't going as well as they would like, but don't know where the problem lies or what to do. As you will see in this chapter, processes are very important and addressing this fundamental area will be a powerful tool for the manager.

Why Look at the Processes?

Processes define how tasks in the organization are to be completed, and whether they are done by one person or several hundred people across several locations, processes need to be done correctly and consistently. Organizations will, of course, have processes; but how well they are designed, documented, and communicated determines how efficiently an organization can run, and that translates into bottom-line performance of the organization. Within some organizations, performance might be assessed in terms of how departments such as manufacturing, inventory control, and shipping are managed, but in other organizations, performance could be defined in areas such as product mix, sales and marketing. This is where organizations can lose on the bottom line and struggle with their profitability or ability to compete in the areas of performance and delivery, without knowing why they can't be more successful.

Poor process performance can occur at all levels in the organization in small or large tasks, but they usually go undetected as being "just the way we've always done it." It is here we see the first sign of a systemic problem built into any organization that doesn't monitor its processes or can't see inefficiency in a process. Sadly enough, in too many cases blame is placed in the wrong area and the problem is not addressed correctly, if at all. This is where care has to be taken in fixing the process because there has to be an accurate assessment of the details within the process to ascertain what is wrong. The manager should look at six general areas of a process that can point to where a problem might be:

1. **Developing the process**—How was the process designed to be done?

2. **Documenting the process**—What form can capture how the process is to be done?

3. **Staffing the process**—Are the correct people performing the process tasks?

4. **Monitoring and measuring the process**—How is the process actually being performed?

5. **Changing the process**—Does the process need improvement or alterations?

6. **Finding other ways**—Are there other ways to accomplish the task that might be more efficient?

As you will see, there are several things that can create poor performance in processes.

Power Tool

The manager needs to know how to *objectively determine what is wrong* in order to *effectively correct problems.* Making these types of assessments and possible adjustments in the organization brings both the manager and the organization to a higher level of performance.

Process Development

As organizations are broken up into functional areas such as accounting, human resources, engineering, sales and marketing, procurements, manufacturing, inventory, and shipping and receiving, each has tasks that will need to be performed, but who will determine how these tasks are done?

Warning

This is the first area in which a problem can arise—the issue of who developed the steps detailing how to accomplish tasks in the department. Depending on the size of the organization and the complexity of the tasks, managers need to have some background on how the processes were developed for their department.

In large organizations, process development teams might have done sophisticated analysis and testing and developed sound and efficient processes, whereas other processes might have been developed by the person assigned the task with little or no analysis done. In either case, tasks were developed and the manager should look into how and why they are being done in a particular way.

Warning

The second problem area can be overly zealous managers who feel the need to change things without knowing the details of why processes are being performed in a certain way. This can be just as damaging as a poorly developed process. Not *all* processes *need* to be changed even if they are old processes.

We are looking into why a process has to be developed and the best practices for developing processes. Process development starts with understanding what has to be accomplished in the department and how a process fits in the overall flow of work being done. The following steps help outline how you develop a process:

1. **Determine a need**—This usually starts with some basic questions about the need for a process. Why does the proposed task have to be done? Is there only one occurrence of the task or is this going to be a repetitive task? Is the task being done in the correct department? Will it be performed by human or mechanical resources or a combination of both? Outline the scope of the process, including all tasks and resources that will be included in the process. Create a proposal of this process to submit to higher management for approval.

2. **Select the person best qualified to correctly develop the process**—Having a good process starts with having the right people developing the process. This can be the start of problems seen in processes and will be important in developing new processes. To clarify, there are those who have critical information about the tasks (subject matter experts) and those who will develop the best way to accomplish what has to be done (process developers). Both are needed and they might or might not be the same person. The important thing is having the most accurate information about the tasks and someone who is skilled in process development. Process developers take information about tasks and develop the best sequence of work to create an efficient flow of tasks that define the process.

3. **Observe the environment in which the process will be conducted**—Care must be taken to understand what effect the new process will have on the existing environment and whether there will be anything in the environment that will present a challenge in developing the new process. Although processes can be developed in a different location to define the steps, it is critical that the process be performed in the location and environment in which it will be conducted to ensure that there are no influences that might alter the process or anything in the process that will have an effect on the surrounding area.

4. **Perform the process**—If this is a new process, it will need to be outlined and the individual steps tested. If this is an existing process, each task and the sequence of tasks should be observed and evaluated by both the subject matter expert and a process developer.

5. **Test the process**—After observations have been made and the process appears to be designed on paper, it is time to test the sequence of tasks. This will be done in both a new process and an existing process because there might be changes that need to be tested. This is where you see whether the process will accomplish the desired output.

6. **Make adjustments and fine-tune**—Now that the process has been verified through testing, it's time to refine the process to make it efficient and cost-effective. Look for ways to streamline the sequence of tasks to make it as efficient as you can.

7. **Test the final revision of the process**—After all the refinements have been made, test the final revision of the process to verify the sequence, speed, accuracy, quality, and desired output to see whether the process is at its best. Try to test the final version in the actual environment to make sure you have accounted for everything that could influence the process.

8. **Document the process**—Now that the process has been verified and tested, the next important part is documenting the
   process. This is where the sequences of tasks in the final version
   are recorded along with any details or instructions that would
   help someone not familiar with the process perform it. Documenting a process is best done by someone experienced in writing process documents because there are certain formats and
   protocols that help promote effective communication of the
   process in written form. After the steps have been recorded,
   the document must be tested. We will cover documenting a
   process in more detail in the next section.

9. **Communicate and train**—The next important step is communicating the process using the document and training. This
   is where the document is tested to see how complete and accurate it is and how easy it will be to follow. When training, use
   well-written documents, let the document do the talking, and
   interject only when needed if something is unclear. Too much
   information during this time can overwhelm the trainee, causing her to struggle. In most cases it is best to "show" how the
   process is done by walking through the document once, and
   then have the trainee "do" the process to get a hands-on feel
   of how it is done, also using the document as a guide. Have
   the trainee perform the process several times without help to
   ensure that she is following the "documented way" and that she
   understands each step. Repetitive training also promotes memory retention and allows the trainee to formulate more advanced
   questions to be answered if needed before the trainee actually
   starts performing the process live. It is important for the trainer
   to be convinced that the trainee knows the process as designed
   before starting because this is where bad habits can start and
   processes might turn out to be not as efficient as they could be.

10. **Monitor and measure process performance**—After the process is in place and running live, there must be a level of monitoring in place to measure how well a process is working. This can be done two ways, measuring each task in the sequence or just measuring the output of the process. In the development stage of the process, measurements were taken to verify the process and these can be used again in verifying the ongoing performance of the process. This is how processes are controlled; they have to be monitored and measured against a goal. Things that can be measured include speed, quality or accuracy, quantity, and cost.

11. **Conduct process improvement if needed**—If measurements indicate that a process is deviating from a baseline or standard, adjustments must be made. Processes will fall into two categories: in control, when the process is performing as expected at peak efficiency, and out of control, when measurements indicate that too much deviation is taking place, resulting in less than desired output. In the latter case, adjustments are needed to bring the process back in control. Care must be taken when making adjustments because more damage than good can result from incorrect adjustments. Remember, this process was designed and verified to be at peak efficiency, so there might be only a small step that is not correct in the process. Always start with observing every step in the process and comparing the steps to the document to ensure that the process is still being done correctly. In most cases there is a step that is not being followed, and this is a simple training fix. In other cases there might be something that has changed, and this might be a good time to bring the subject matter expert *and* the process developer back in to see where the problem exists and to get recommendations on what adjustment is needed. In either case, verify that the process has been brought back into control and is performing per the document and as expected, and continue to monitor and measure performance.

One note of importance in process integrity is that all too often we have a tendency to blame people for problems that occur in the operation. People are doing their job and in many cases following a process, but this is where problems can exist. If the person is following a process but the process is not good, the outcome will be failure.

Power Tool

In troubleshooting a process problem, one should be focusing not on *the person* as being the problem but more on *the process* as being the problem.

There might have been poor training, or lack of an established process, and people are left to decide on their own how to perform the task. The manager must look at process problems and improvement with an open mind, evaluating the design of the process, the documentation, and the ability of the staff to perform the process correctly.

In some cases tasks are performed based on tribal knowledge, or information passed down through the ranks and over time. This can be problematic because this information is not documented and analyzed but simply is passed down over time. The people who are communicating this information and their skills in communication and training will determine the quality of the information that's being passed on.

Some people are very good at articulating process details and can train people very well. Other people might be an expert in a particular process but not necessarily good at training or communicating process steps. This can lead to confusion and misunderstanding or steps that are left out because the trainer assumes that the trainee already knows the information. This will lead to two directions of process control: The first relates to the documentation process itself and the second relates to how the processes are being communicated and trained within the organization.

Documentation

Documentation is vital within an organization and it must be taken seriously if the organization is to succeed. Documentation as it relates to processes is important because it defines how things are designed to be done. How documentation is developed, recorded, and used in training is also vital. As you have seen, problems can occur due to a misunderstanding of the process steps, or due to processes being developed incorrectly or not at all, resulting in several layers of problems. The first step in looking into fixing problems involves looking at the documentation and in some cases this might shed some light as to why there are fundamental problems with a process. It might not be the process itself but more a lack of proper documentation of the process that can lead to poor training or inconsistency in process steps and sequence. Documentation is the foundation of processes performed in the organization, and it must be written correctly for the organization to operate at its highest efficiency.

The writing of a process document should involve two types of resources, the subject matter expert (with knowledge of the process steps) and the process developer (skilled in process development and document writing).

Warning

A document written by a subject matter expert might have parts of the process omitted because the writer might *assume* a certain level of knowledge by the reader. Document writers *need to assume that the reader has never performed the process* so every step, in detail, must be included.

The next step is to select someone who has no knowledge of the process and have them perform it using only your document and no help of any kind. If the person can perform the process steps correctly, using the document without help (including verbal queues), then the process is well documented. The purpose of well-documented processes is to effectively communicate the process details when needed.

For processes that have been documented, one needs to look at and read through them to see whether they make logical sense. This should be done by two people: the subject matter expert (someone who is very familiar with the process) and the process developer who designed the process. After they have read through the process, they should take the document and go to the area within the organization where the process is carried out and have one or more individuals walk through the process to see whether it matches the document. It might be discovered that a process was documented very well, but the people doing the process are doing it differently than described in the document. In some cases the resources performing the process steps are actually doing it correctly and this might have changed over time as a result of process improvement, but this change simply was not documented. In other cases, modifications were made to the process documents but were never communicated to those doing the process. In either case the process will be prone to failure if information about a process is not properly documented so that it can be communicated to others unfamiliar with the process.

The manager might need to consider the perception of what is being done by management outside the department. Management might be aware of a process as defined several years ago, but not be aware of current changes made to the process and thus might question what is being done. This is usually a result of poor or incomplete documentation change control—such that changes are made with little or no communication. Many problems with processes can be related to areas of process control, document control, and a document change or update system. With as much work as there is invested in process development, there can be just as many problems arising from documentation.

Staffing a Process

Now that you have evaluated the process steps; properly documented, reviewed, and tested the process improvements; and are convinced that you have the best possible design, you have to look at the resources you have in place to perform these processes. Although you have a great process in place, even the best process isn't going to be effective if you don't have the correct people performing the process. Not everyone can do every process efficiently. You have to consider the skill set of the people you've chosen for a process and match that skill set with what's required in order to perform the process effectively.

Power Tool

Having people *doing jobs they are skilled at and educated for* allows the organization to best utilize its resources and promotes job satisfaction.

Managers need to monitor their staff, their needs, and whether they are successful in the assignments they are given because this can play a large role in the success of processes. Managers should be able to tell if a resource is not performing well and should meet with that resource to determine whether the problem is work related and what steps can be taken to address the issue. It might be that the resource has not been fully trained on the process, or that the resources does not have all the tools or work environment needed to perform that process. It could also be that the resource simply does not have all the skills required to perform the process and needs to be replaced.

Managers should also look at all the processes being performed in their department to see who they have assigned to each process. There might be some resources who are skilled in several areas and could do many processes, whereas other resources might only be able to do certain processes well. Mangers typically want to staff their department with as many multiskilled resources as possible to have the flexibility in resource leveling, but this isn't always the case; managers do have to hand-select some resources for certain processes. As skill is one part of the resource allocation equation, numbers of resources also play a role in resource staffing.

Part of process design lies in ensuring that you have the correct number of people doing the process and will not be overburdened with a lack of resources or become complacent from having too many resources, which can promote failure and mistakes. In most cases, capacity modeling for processes will indicate the resource loading required to balance processes in a department. This involves determining how long the process takes compared to other processes being performed in the department and leveling resources to accomplish everything that needs to be done in a given timeframe. The manager has a limited number of resources and needs to accomplish a set amount of work, so the resources need to be scheduled to cover all the work required but not be overallocated.

Power Tool

A large part of this scheduling dilemma involves having the *right staff doing the processes they are training and skilled for.* Scheduling techniques are covered in more detail in Chapter 5, "Managing Your Resources."

Training Staff for Processes

Having processes designed as efficiently as possible and having the staff with the skills to perform a process are two critical steps. The third step is properly training the staff. Without training, resources are left to begin a process by interpreting a document or starting with little or no guidance. Someone needs to communicate the proper steps in the correct sequence and have the resource perform the process to ensure that they fully understand what they are doing. This requires a person not only qualified to perform the process, but also skilled in training. Managers must consider who has been assigned the task of training staff within the organization because their skill set and ability to train people is critical. Just because someone is an expert at a process does not mean they are the best person to train that process. In some cases they might be, but it all depends on the person and how she can effectively communicate the task's steps to somebody who has never performed that task.

After you have chosen the trainers, you need to consider the training environment and how many staff will be trained at one time. When training is completed, the test of that training will require the measuring system discussed earlier. As with process improvement, new people will be performing these tasks for the first time and will need to be assessed as to whether they are effective in performing those tasks. This comes from measuring their performance against the baseline or expectation for that process.

Care must be taken to properly assess new staff members' performance on a process because they will not be able to perform the tasks as quickly and efficiently as more experienced people. Allow the person time to become comfortable in doing the process, and as they build confidence, their performance will improve. If too much pressure is put on the individual to perform too soon in the learning stage, this can present the opportunity for failure. Establish a reasonable amount of time for resources to learn a process, and communicate that expectation as a goal to reach.

Power Tool

When *quality training* has been accomplished and processes are being completed efficiently, it will be a form of completion that gives the department and manager power.

Monitoring and Measuring a Process

When management wants to assess the effectiveness or efficiency of a process, there needs to be some way of measuring the process. Depending on the process, there can be several ways you can measure such things as scope, quality, quantity, and general efficiency. When you are considering the measurement of a process, there has to be a monitoring system in place to gather information. In the process of monitoring and measuring, there are certain steps that need to be considered:

1. Review what the *original intent* of the process was (scope, quality, quantity).

2. Review the *tested results* from the design phase of the process.

3. Form a *standard or baseline* from the data in the design of the process.

4. *Collect data* on the current process to document performance.

5. *Compare current data* to the baseline and identify variances.

6. *Prioritize the variances* in a Pareto chart from highest to lowest.

7. Develop a plan to *address each issue* in the process.

8. *Measure any changes* that have been made to verify performance.

9. *Update documentation* and *retrain staff* on changes.

In the general understanding of monitoring and measuring, what the manager is actually developing is a process of control. If processes are left to run unchecked or monitored, there is no way to quantify process efficiency or even success. The process of measuring and collection process data is called statistical process control (SPC). There are tools that managers can use to gather and analyze data to understand the general performance of processes and any problems or inefficiencies that actually occur. Following are several SPC-type tools that can be found in text and on the Internet:

- Check charts
- X-Bar, R charts
- Pareto charts
- Histogram
- Scatter diagram

One simple tool for gathering information is the *check chart*. A check chart can be set up in a couple of ways:

1. Use a list of process steps and record data for each time the step is completed, such as times, quantity, or the use of certain items.

2. Record the problems that occur at each process step, such as pass or fail, quality issues that are found, etc.

Tables 3.1 and 3.2 show some examples of how check charts can be set up to record data.

Table 3.1 Check Chart to Record Process Step Problems

Process Name:			Date:	Staff Name:
Process Step	Scheduled Time	Actual Time	Pass/Fail	Rework Required
1a	30 min	26 min	Pass	
1b	90 min	91 min	Pass	
1c	45 min	57 min	Fail	Rework required
2a	120 min	122 min	Pass	
2b	90 min	90 min	Pass	
3a	40 min	67 min	Fail	Rework required
3b	25 min	22 min	Pass	
3c	60 min	66 min	Pass	
3d	35 min	35 min	Pass	
4a	30 min	52 min	Fail	Rework required
4b	15 min	16 min	Pass	
4c	45 min	44 min	Pass	

Table 3.2 Check Chart to Record Problems on Specific Items

Process Name: 1a		Date:	Staff Name:
Serial Number	Time Duration	Pass/Fail	Rework Required
BN22314	67 min	Pass	
BN22315	66 min	Pass	
BN22316	67 min	Pass	
BN22317	92 min	Fail	Rework required
BN22318	65 min	Pass	
BN22319	66 min	Pass	
BN22320	66 min	Pass	
BN22321	21 min	Fail	Rework required
BN22322	65 min	Pass	
BN22323	66 min	Pass	
BN22324	27 min	Fail	Rework required
BN22325	65 min	Pass	

Simple designators that show or qualify how a process step was performed can record how a process is actually being done and reveal even minor issues happening at each step. The use of check charts is valuable to gather any amount or type of information that you want. When check charts are used throughout a process, information can be gathered on a daily or weekly basis and put into a spreadsheet that shows what the outcome of that process actually is. When you have a way of collecting data, you can see how the process steps are being carried out, and their effectiveness and efficiency become visible quite easily. In some cases there might be different people doing a process, or the process might be done by several people over multiple shifts. This will also be valuable information, as you can see, if the process changes depending on the people, the shift, or time of day. This is information that can be looked at and analyzed to see whether any process improvements need to be made.

Now that information has been gathered as to how the process is being conducted, the data needs to be analyzed to evaluate the process. Real-time process data needs to be compared to standard or original design criteria to see whether there are variations in how it is being conducted against the original design. Using the data from how the process was originally designed or intended is called *setting a baseline*. Compare the baseline to the actual data you gathered and see where problems or deviations from the intended process are occurring. This is a powerful tool because slight changes usually occur that can point to problems or inefficiencies.

This is also a great opportunity to remind those involved in the process how the process was originally intended to be done. Subtle changes are not always visible while a process is being observed, but when the process is compared to the baseline, obvious differences could account for inefficiencies. In some cases managers look at problems or deviations as not following the process and decide that this is why processes are failing, but managers should be careful in analyzing data to understand what the deviations are actually uncovering.

You might be simply verifying that a process is actually being done correctly compared to the baseline. In other cases you might also verify that a process is being done incorrectly and modifications need to be made. This might lead to more training or better documentation and communication of how the process steps are to be carried out. The data might indicate that something in the environment surrounding the process needs to be addressed. Within an organization, managers should be monitoring processes being carried out to ensure that the business is running most effectively and efficiently. Managers should also understand any deviations from the baseline and act quickly to address issues that might arise. The data might indicate a problem that, if left unattended, will result in loss of time, material, quality, and resource availability.

One area to consider when managers want to change something in a process is any reluctance by the people doing the process to change. This is common and usually is a result of people having done a process for a very long time, in a particular way, and they think that's the only way to do the process—or they simply do not like change. This might also be from people who have altered a process based on the way they "see" that a process should be done and it's not being done as it has been documented. In either case, it's the responsibility of the manager to oversee the processes within the assigned area and to ensure that processes are being done correctly and look for ways to improve processes.

Managers should pay attention and listen to the resources doing these processes because these individuals work with the process and have very good input and ideas about improvements that would make the process more efficient.

Power Tool

The resources performing tasks within the process can sometimes *spot subtle changes* not captured in the data and can *improve a process*.

Even small changes to a process add up over several processes in the organization and can result in significant improvements in efficiency. In regularly monitoring and measuring processes, managers should ask those doing the process whether there's any way the process can be improved. This gives the manager an opportunity to have more contact with the resources in the organization and better understand the process from the workers' perspective. It will also improve the credibility of the manager because the people will see that he is truly interested in the work being performed and wants to make sure that work is being done most efficiently. This is also seen when process improvement ideas originating from the resources are actually implemented, allowing them to feel a sense of ownership of the process and to feel that they were able to have a part in making it better.

Changing the Process

Now that you have a way of measuring a process and analyzing the process performance, there needs to be a way of making a change if needed. The area of process improvement is very important within an organization because it involves implementing a change to an existing process, allowing it to be more effective, have better quality, or improve efficiency. This is one area managers in which can have a big impact within the organization, by ensuring that all the processes being performed in their area are at peak efficiency. They can determine this through data-gathering tools and analysis that pinpoints what areas can use improvement. Managers must ask themselves whether a process *needs* to be changed, why it's being changed, and what they plan to gain from this change.

As you have already seen, changes to a process can actually result in its getting better or possibly getting worse, so when changes are made, they need to be remeasured and reanalyzed to ensure that the change actually accomplished the desired outcome. When a change is being considered, there needs to be a plan (process) to document and control the activities needed to develop the change. The change should be evaluated off-line so as not to interrupt the normal process. If it is not possible to test the change off-line, the manager must schedule some downtime so that the change can be tested. Changes should be made only by resources qualified in process development to correctly outline the change parameters, test conditions, and documentation. Changes can be tested in two general ways:

1. **Designed and calculated**—Designed changes are when someone has developed a modification and documented how the change will be tested and implemented.

2. **On-the-fly**—On-the-fly changes are ideas tested in the current process environment to meet a more immediate need with the intent that the change will be implemented quickly.

The biggest difference is in preparation and the ability to perform adequate and thorough testing prior to implementation. Both require testing the change first to verify the desired effect, documenting the change, and training resources performing the process on the new change.

When considering a change to a process, one generally has an idea that they think will produce a desired outcome but, when tried, results in a different outcome than expected. This might require a trial-and-error type of approach in which small modifications to the process can be made until the desired outcome is actually achieved. After you have consistently shown that the desired outcome can be achieved with this process improvement, the change needs to be documented. When a change has been permanently made and documented, the change then needs to be communicated to all involved with the process. This is where potential problems usually lie in process improvement—perhaps someone was able to make an effective change but it was poorly documented or communicated and therefore the change does not take its full effect. When change has been communicated to those performing the process, measuring this process again has to be done to ensure that the change is still producing the desired outcome and that the desired outcome is being achieved by all who are performing the process. This will ensure that the change is sustainable and will produce the efficiency desired in the change.

Is There a Better Way?

As you have seen, processes are used to accomplish things in the organization, and how these processes are designed, grouped, and carried out plays an important role in the success of the organization. The manager should look at two primary levels concerning process organization:

1. **High level**—Look at the entire department as a whole and all the processes being performed. Determine whether they all belong in that department and are grouped or organized correctly.

2. **Low level**—Look at each process individually by monitoring and measuring to determine whether each process is running as it was designed and at its highest efficiency.

The organization of processes can be just as important as the process design itself. The manager must evaluate not only what processes they have, but where they are located, and how they are grouped and interact with each other. The manager should ask the questions, why do we have these processes, are there any other ways to perform the processes, and can we split processes into smaller components or simplify tasks to make them easier and reduce errors? Managers, in monitoring their department, need to continually ask themselves whether the overall department is running as efficiently as it can.

Processes that feed other processes are important to evaluate because this interface can be difficult sometimes. One side is viewed as the supplier (delivering the product) and the other side is seen as the customer (accepting the product). The evaluation would be to determine whether the product being delivered is complete, is meeting the quality standard, and is on time. The only way each process group will be successful is if each is starting the process with everything they need and delivering the output as expected. This *process integration* needs to be measured, much like measuring the individual processes, to verify that it is being completed as designed. Evaluating this data against a standard or baseline will help the manager determine whether changes are needed in the interfaces or groups of processes.

In this macro view of the department's processes, it's important to remember that any changes need to be carefully designed and tested before they are implemented. This is another area that can cause as many problems as it solves if not done correctly. The manager needs to expand her thinking this time to a larger scale, including the idea of which department should be doing each process, or where in the process lineup all the processes fall, and whether the lineup is correct. Be prepared to discover that some processes might not even be needed anymore or can be modified to they point where they can be combined with another process. This does require thinking out-of-the-box about what "really" needs to be done to accomplish the desired output of the department. The manager now has tools to effectively evaluate the department and make necessary changes in both individual processes and the overall organization of the department. This is one of the many ways you will see how organizations continually improve profitability and maintain a competitive advantage in the marketplace.

Power Tool Summary

- *Defined processes* should be found all throughout the organization and should be documented to record and communicate how series of tasks are designed and sequenced to complete a process.

- The manager needs to know how to *objectively determine what is wrong* in order to *effectively correct problems.* Making these types of assessments and possible adjustments in the organization brings both the manager and the organization to a higher level of performance.

- In troubleshooting a process problem, one should be focusing not on *the person* as being the problem but more on *the process* as being the problem.

- Having people *doing jobs they are skilled at and educated for* allows the organization to best utilize its resources and promotes job satisfaction.

- A large part of this scheduling dilemma involves having the *right staff doing the processes they are training and skilled for.* Scheduling techniques are covered in more detail in Chapter 5.

- When *quality training* has been accomplished and processes are being completed efficiently, it will be a form of completion that gives the department and manager power.

- The resources performing tasks within the process can sometimes *spot subtle changes* not captured in the data and can *improve a process.*

4

Waste Management

What Is Waste in an Organization?

Organizations spend hundreds of thousands of dollars needlessly each year on things that didn't really need to be done, as a result of some anomaly falsely creating the need. So how do these "anomalies" occur and how can managers spot them and reduce or eliminate the problems? Anomalies, in this context, might be seen as things done out of the norm, workarounds, or mishaps, but what is not seen are the problems embedded in the system that go undetected. This is where anomalies turn into waste as they are designed into the system, go undetected, and fail to be identified, reduced, and eliminated. Managers should be continually looking for ways to improve processes to make their department more efficient, and another way to accomplish that task is through identifying and eliminating waste.

Waste can come in several forms, all throughout the organization, from poor time management to incorrect resources assigned to tasks, insufficient documentation, poorly designed processes, hiccups in supply chain, and many other areas that have a "bad" spot in the process and generate waste. In this chapter we will look at some specific areas in the operation such as human resources, process organization, departmental staffing, manufacturing, facilities, and managerial organization that are typically culprits in waste generation.

When we consider how to approach organizational improvements by reducing or eliminating waste, the fundamental thought process will require a project management philosophy of Streamline Thinking.

Power Tool

Streamline Thinking requires evaluating the *minimum requirement to get from start to completion* and stripping away everything else that is not critical to the minimum requirement.

This will be very difficult because it demands the evaluator to *think outside of the box* and away from an established paradigm for a normal everyday process in the department. This can be uncomfortable because there will be some changes affecting only processes, materials, or equipment, whereas other changes could lead to movement or elimination of human resources, which can be very difficult. It is important to understand the difference between *waste* and *inefficiency*.

Waste refers to parts of a process that are simply not needed or are overstaffed, or things that can be eliminated without affecting the outcome of the process. Inefficiency refers to areas that are "needed" but require improvement to be better and could affect the outcome of a process. In either case, an evaluation should be done to assess the documented process against the actual process for unnecessary things that can be eliminated. The manager should be looking not only at the components of each task, but also the need for each task, as well as the staff needed, at a minimum, to complete the tasks. The manager might solicit the resources doing the tasks for their opinion as well as a process developer for ideas on areas that can be removed.

Process Organization

When we look at waste management in accomplishing process tasks, there are generally two areas: physical items relative to the task and the human resources assigned to perform the tasks. It is important for the manager to properly evaluate each area because false assumptions can be made as to who or what is at fault in creating waste. The Streamline Thinking approach takes much of the guesswork out and puts the emphasis on *what doesn't belong* in the evaluation. It's also good to try to be as objective as possible in this evaluation to make sure that there is no bias to task improvement over human resource reduction because this can be a very difficult decision.

Task Evaluation

When a manager is evaluating items in a task, it is best to review the documentation on how the process was designed. The manager could do this along with a process developer to review the document looking for signs of waste. The process developer might look at the document through different eyes than the manager and might see areas of waste that the manager can't see, or vice versa. Remember to use Streamline Thinking because it will reveal things that are not needed (waste) and allow the manager to focus on the core requirements of the process. It's also important for the manager to realize that he is evaluating a process he might see happening on a regular basis and it will be difficult to spot waste because it looks normal or needed. This is why it's important to have a process developer or the subject matter expert help evaluate.

Task evaluation requires a keen eye on the details of each task in the process. The evaluator must ask herself *why each part of the task is there* and *whether it is required* in the overall outcome of the process. This is critical because there might have been unneeded steps added in the design phase or steps added later that really are not needed to accomplish the desired output, and *this is waste.* Look at the details of each task step and you might find small things that are being done that are not necessary and waste time and material. People performing tasks in a process sometimes add little steps that are not necessary and add time (waste). Focus on the things being done, the materials used, and why each part of the current process is being done, and you will usually find things that can be eliminated. Remember, everything that is used costs money and every minute that is spent costs time and money; so determine what the minimum requirement is to complete each task in the process and make sure that it is as lean and efficient as possible.

Human Resource Evaluation

Evaluating human resources in a department has to be broken down into two primary areas: skills/abilities and the number of staff needed to perform all the duties in the department. The manager needs to be clear about the objectives of this type of evaluation. Reduce *waste,* not manpower!

Power Tool

The *resources in the department are valuable* and would not be there if they weren't skilled and needed; it just needs to be determined where they are best utilized.

If there are resources who are highly skilled and there are assigned tasks not utilizing their skills, the organization is wasting those resources. The organization has the resources available, but is simply not using them to the fullest benefit to the organization. If a resource is doing tasks utilizing her skills, those tasks are performed at higher efficiency and the resource is not being wasted within the organization. Other resources not skilled for tasks to which they are assigned might be struggling or performing at a lower efficiency, but it could be that they are skilled in other tasks to which they are not assigned—this also is a wasted resource within the organization. This is where the manager needs to identify the difference between wasted utilization of resources and poor efficiency in processes.

The difference is in how the manager views human resources in the department. Human resources viewed at the process level would be seen as efficient or not (process efficiency), whereas resources viewed at the organizational level would see poor skill-set utilization as wasting good resources on bad assignments (resource waste). This is the kind of waste we want to eliminate within the department and organization. This does not mean a reduction in workforce, just an evaluation of the skills that resources have against the task assignments they are given.

Power Tool

Making adjustments to optimize resources both reduces waste in poor resource allocation and improves process efficiency by utilizing the best skill sets, making this a power tool for the manager.

With the evaluation of processes and resource utilization, the number of staff will probably be evaluated as well, and the manager can determine whether the department has the correct number of human resources. It might be determined that there are some processes that simply have too many resources assigned, and a reduction of staff could improve the cost overhead of a process.

Warning

When a manager is making the judgment of how many human resources are needed, it is best to go back to the design of the process to see what the minimum requirements were to avoid understaffing a process and creating stress.

Processes are generally designed to be staffed at the optimum, but can acquire more resources over time for any number of reasons. This is why a periodic review of staff used in the department is needed in order to avoid overstaffing and waste.

The other part of this warning in evaluating staff reduction, when there's no economic downturn, would be streamlining the organization by eliminating resources when it's apparent that they are not necessary, or at least when the perception within the organization suggests that they're not necessary. Resources might question management's motives for arbitrarily laying off people, resulting in others in the department having to take on more responsibility, and might wonder why this has to be the case. In an economic downturn, staff reduction is typically viewed as a temporary endeavor to reduce cost, and most staff in the organization understand what is happening and why. In this case, management is obviously intending to streamline the organization, which puts an incredible strain on the remaining staff because this does not appear to be a short-term endeavor. This might result in people leaving if they do not agree with the work environment that has been created as a result. So streamlining your processes to reduce waste might result in cost reduction as well as a reduction in workforce. You have to be careful about balancing this against overstressing the workforce and having them take on too many responsibilities, which is not sustainable!

Waste or Manufacturing Cost Reductions?

Areas in the organization that are more complicated—involving difficult processes and complex dynamics—present opportunities for generating waste. Departments such as engineering, manufacturing, and inventory control are examples of areas rich in potential waste. As you have seen, waste can be seen as things "not needed" to meet minimum requirements, so reducing or eliminating this waste might be in the form of cost reduction and process improvement.

Engineering is a difficult department to evaluate because there might not be as many "set" processes defining how to accomplish tasks. Much of engineering is based on first-level prototype, trial-and-error-type processes, making it a great place to evaluate waste generation. Here are some things to consider when evaluating waste in a department like engineering:

- Number of resources assigned to tasks
- Supplies and materials bought for prototypes
- Equipment being brought in to test prototypes
- Software being purchased and the question of whether the group will use it beyond that project
- Floor and office space being used

Departments like engineering can have a tendency to overspend in these areas because they want to make sure that they have enough to cover what is needed; however, in many cases, too much is purchased out of habit, and this process needs to be checked to reduce further waste.

Power Tool

Evaluating how many resources are used on which projects ensures that projects are covered and skill sets are assigned correctly to maximize efficiency.

Manufacturing is an area with lots of opportunities for generating waste, and because there are many areas within manufacturing, this can also be a place to hide waste just as easily. In manufacturing, two primary areas of purchasing take place:

1. **Manufacturing product**—This is all product and materials purchased that "go into products" manufactured for the organization to sell.

2. **Manufacturing support**—This is all equipment, fixtures, machines, and anything required to "assist in manufacturing" products.

Product and materials that go into making up the final product to be sold are generally seen as waste free because the bill of materials is well defined and only what is needed is purchased. Two main areas of waste in manufactured products are too much inventory purchased and stored using valuable storage space, and excess inventory to address rework stuck in process. This is an example of "hidden" waste because the "rework stuck in process" area is difficult to measure and manage new versus old inventory. You don't know the waste is there until you measure and expose it.

Manufacturing support, on the other hand, is much like engineering, in which there can be lots of waste in areas like resource allocation, special materials for fixtures, and testing that don't get used or that get used once and never again. Time can also be wasted in manufacturing engineering when the engineers are not very efficient with the projects or testing that they are working on. Statistical process measurements need to be done and are very important, but that process needs to be streamlined, efficient, and generally trained and managed by good leadership. This can be another area where waste is "hidden" because the manager might not know what the minimum time requirements are, so he also will not know how much time is wasted.

Waste in Procurement

Companies purchase things to use in the operation, for distribution and sales, or to be used in products that are manufactured and sold by the organization. How this is done can play a big role in managing not only efficiency in the department but also cash flow in the organization. Most procurement offices have a preferred vendor/supplier list, but this should be backed up with an analysis of why one would be chosen over another. This can be done with a tool called a Suppler Analysis Matrix as shown in Table 4.1.

Table 4.1 Supplier Analysis Matrix, Example

Vendor/ Supplier	Price	Quality	Stock Available	On-Time Delivery	Customer Service	Score
A & B Machine	Excellent	Average	Average	Poor	Excellent	17
Central Machine	Poor	Excellent	Average	Excellent	Poor	15
Bay Machine	Average	Poor	Excellent	Average	Poor	13

Power Tool

One tool to evaluate spending is to construct *a Supplier Analysis Matrix.* A supplier analysis looks at both what has to be purchased in the organization and who the qualified suppliers are.

This list, after it has been created, is not carved in stone and it should be reevaluated on a regular basis. Other criteria can be added to customize the matrix. Weights can also be added to criteria that increase the importance of a particular aspect. Suppliers can change over time as a result of problems such as quality, on-time delivery, pricing, and customer service. In some cases, adding or eliminating products might change how the organization does business with that supplier.

Examples of ways a relationship can change might be a supplier having good pricing on the first item it sold in order to get a foot in the door, then switching to a higher price on future items to make up for the profit margin. Another example might be changes in how contracts are structured that introduce new conditions that might be favorable or not for the organization. One area to review is the ability of the purchasing agents to negotiate with suppliers while keeping the best interest of the organization in mind. The buyers can make or break this department, and leadership and training are required here to ensure that procurements are done correctly. If an organization is spending too much on its procurements, this is an area of waste that can be evaluated, and changes can be made to improve spending and eliminate waste.

Waste in Shipping and Receiving

Shipping and receiving is a difficult area in which to manage waste because it's constantly changing with regard to product storage, things being staged for shipping/receiving, and things coming to the facility. The logistics involved in managing this properly and efficiently can get complex, and waste can be both generated and hidden in this area. This can be difficult to evaluate because those working in shipping/receiving understand the current design of the department and might have difficulty seeing a better, more efficient way. This might require getting someone from outside the department or hiring a consultant to come in and evaluate the area for waste and improvements. Shipping/receiving needs to be viewed as a transitional area through which things move and where they do not stay very long. Waste will be in two forms: how long items stay (occupying space) and what equipment (tools and equipment, tables, racks and shelves, and so on) are needed for "transition" or "storage" of items.

This area in the facility costs money and should not be long-term storage for items that should be located somewhere else (hidden waste). If most of the space and equipment is used for transition and the layout is efficient, that is good. If the layout has excessive amounts of floor space used for storage or "nontransitional" purposes, that might be waste and might need to be evaluated. There needs to be a separation between inefficiency and waste, because efficiency includes things that are needed in the process but just require improvement, and waste includes things identified as not needed that therefore can be eliminated. Having an outside set of eyes to evaluate the area helps leads to more objectivity about what really is part of the process and needs to be there.

Waste in Facilities

Organizations spend hundreds of millions of dollars each year on buildings around the world for warehousing, manufacturing, office space, gathering space, and convention space to conduct business. The cost of space varies depending on what it is used for; for example, a large open warehouse space is much less expensive than built-out office space with lots of office walls, restrooms, and expensive lobbies. Organizations are willing to spend extra money on facilities where it counts, when the facilities either are needed or will yield a return based on strategic design.

Facilities have more of a tendency to store waste than to generate waste because the facility itself is not usually associated with a specific process, but simply facilitates processes. Many organizations overbuy on the size of the facility for growth, and then fill it up and use all the space right from the start, building in waste. Utilizing the extra space is not a bad thing; it's when the space usage turns permanent that it can become waste. This can be done from long-term planning strategies in which executive management is planning for growth potential in order to take advantage of current real estate pricing, and large areas of the building might not be utilized but are intended to be utilized later as the organization grows and expands. This is an acceptable strategy because you are able to lock in long-term leases on a larger building to get a building while it's available. Some companies might have a smaller building and might have to move to a larger building for expansion later, costing much more on leases and affecting their bottom line, giving your organization an advantage.

Another way to look at space management within a building is to consider how much time the employees spend walking around, going to areas like restrooms, and moving within the department to accomplish normal, everyday tasks. Employees' time spent walking around the building can be a large area of waste that can be evaluated by management and in some cases, can be improved greatly by evaluating the interior layout of the facility. Human resources, in most cases, are some of the most expensive resources in the organization, and if these resources have to spend too much time walking throughout the facility not performing tasks, they are not getting work done for the organization, creating waste. If resources have everything readily available in close proximity, this reduces the amount of walking time, improves efficiency, and can start to eliminate waste.

Waste in Managerial Decision Making

Managerial decision making is important to the organization because decisions have to be discussed, negotiated, and finalized, as well as implemented. In the process of the organization's decision making, several areas within the process can produce waste, such as who was assigned to make the decision, how good the person is at making a decision, and what this person's decision-making process entails. Let's look at who is making a decision and for what reason that person was chosen for a decision. This might be the person in charge of a department or an organization, whose responsibility normally is to make decisions. In other cases, a group or committee will be tasked with making the decision and this sometimes is where problems and waste can occur.

When managers are faced with making a decision, they are actually faced with a process, and in some cases managers lack a process for making decisions. The manager can spend a lot of time gathering information, deliberating about what course of action to take, and deciding what criteria will need to be used in making the decision. Managers can do this intuitively and quickly because they are generally more experienced and confident in their abilities. They also understand the organization and their department, and the needs and requirements for the decision. Faced with a decision, they gather information, formulate a plan, and decide on something quickly and efficiently (no waste). This is good if an organization has managers capable of doing that. Some managers struggle at making some types of decisions, while making other types of decisions very well, and this is typically due to lack of a decision-making process, which creates waste.

Waste in Meetings and Decision Processing

An important area the manager might want to consider when it comes to decision making is waste with regard to meetings. As responsible resources within the organization, managers have to evaluate how many meetings are being conducted, for what reason, the duration, and whether they are justified. Because perception is powerful, the manager might find that resources in the department see managers spending (wasting) time in meetings, and this might result in a reduction in productivity as they feel the need to slow down or take part in a wasted time effort while the manager is gone. A double whammy of wasted time! This is a difficult thing to measure or analyze if it's happening at all.

When managers are visible in their department, productivity seems to increase, but when managers move off to meetings, productivity has a tendency to back off and can generate waste within the department. Managers must manage by example here, because their staff does pay attention to what they are doing, and the staff might send a message to their leader conveying their concern about excessive meetings.

Power Tool

Managers can mitigate this "perception" by *simply communicating* what meetings they "have" to attend and what their part might be. In setting this type of precedent, the *manager is more transparent and the staff might be more understanding* of the manager's plight with meetings.

Decision Processing

When managers make decisions, it usually results in a change in direction, a change of process, or some change affecting the department that will impact human resources in some way. Changes might be small, relatively low-cost, and hardly affecting anyone, but could also be large with a great impact on the department. In any case, decisions force change and need to be evaluated as to whether it has improved or worsened the efficiency of a process or the department. With some organizations, the manager might have to question the decision process itself and the resulting waste a poor decision process can create.

In these types of decisions, there are two elements to consider: time wasted in the decision process itself and waste as a result of a decision that was made. Managers and staff can spend a great deal of time in just the decision-making process. This is usually a result of a lack of or no decision-making process. We know that processes help define and organize tasks to increase efficiency in accomplishing a goal.

Power Tool

To help eliminate waste, a *decision-making process should be developed* to efficiently guide you through a decision.

Decisions are made every day by managers—some resulting in improvements, others resulting in generation of waste. For decisions needed on things currently happening, the manager could revert to the decision-making process that might include an evaluation of new ideas compared to the current way to validate an improvement. For a new process, this might be more difficult because there is nothing to compare it with. In either case, the manager must carefully review decisions to see whether they are creating waste in any way.

One example of good decision making for the manager is in the use of department staff. Because most human resources are responsible for certain processes in the department, their skill is best used in that capacity, and problems can arise if a resource cannot make it to work. The manager has to decide how to resolve this issue: have the process not performed for that day, have someone else perform the process, or perform the process herself. This is a very real scenario that all managers face, making this decision and covering everything that has to be done.

Cross-training is a good way to approach staffing issues. As more and more staff in the department become trained on other areas within the department, the department becomes stronger and the decision process becomes easier, reducing waste. Another byproduct of cross-training is that this allows the manager to evaluate resources in other processes within the department. This might result in seeing skills in a resource that were not known and the resource performing better at a different process than the one he was assigned. Cross-training not only strengthens the department, but also allows the manager to evaluate staffing assignments to ensure that the right skill sets are assigned to the right tasks, reducing waste by redistributing resources and improving efficiency in the department.

On a much higher level in the organization, decisions might need to be considered that evaluate areas such as organizational structure, approach in marketing, sales and product mix, design and layout of each department, and general approach to manufacturing or service. This type of evaluation can be at several levels in the organization, starting as high as the executive branch evaluating the infrastructure of the organization for efficiency and sustainability in the marketplace as well as the effectiveness in accomplishing the strategic business objective. The evaluation can be at the midlevel of management, evaluating the efficiency of each individual department or division with regard to layout, processes, and resource allocation. It is good for the organization to periodically evaluate the operation to ensure that current structuring, design and implementation of processes, and staffing are effectively accomplishing the business objectives.

Sustainable Change

In operations waste management and elimination, we have looked at areas in reducing cost, process improvement, staffing requirements, resource allocation, and decision making to increase productivity and efficiency, but is it sustainable? How sustainable these actions are must be considered by management to validate whether change will result in long-term efficiency. When managers consider change within the organization, it's important to look at what long-term effects the change will have because that will gauge how sustainable that change will actually be.

One common type of change might be staff reduction as a way of reducing overhead costs. This type of change comes with a price because the process tasks have not gone away, but will now have to be done with fewer staff. This work environment results in short-term gain, but might not be sustainable.

Power Tool

In designing sustainable change in cost reduction, the manager might find that he can *eliminate a process or combine a process* with another, allowing for a reduction in staff. This not only *eliminates waste* but *creates positive sustainable change.*

Another efficient way to address staffing issues is to redistribute staff to other parts of the organization. Staff can be moved from one department and reassigned to another department that actually needs that skill set. This is difficult because the need for increased staff in the other department has to be analyzed to ensure that it is justified;

you don't want to simply be shifting resources around. This type of analytical approach to change should be used no matter what kinds of changes are being evaluated. Changes a manager makes in his department might affect other departments negatively, so the manager must keep an open mind as to whether the changes will be in the best interest of the organization and not just his department.

As you have seen, waste can exist all throughout the organization and at all levels within the organization. Waste can be very obvious, out in the open screaming to be addressed, as well as hidden in processes, facilities, and poor or no decision process or planning. Waste does cost organizations millions of dollars every year and sadly it often goes unchecked year after year. The manager must be looking for waste if she is going to address it. Waste must always be seen as "not needed" so it can be eliminated if possible. Dealing with waste can be difficult sometimes because hard decisions might have to be made to address what to do with it. If the manager can view waste as costing the organization time, money, or resources, she has a much better chance of identifying solutions to reduce or eliminate waste.

Power Tool Summary

- Streamline Thinking requires evaluating the *minimum requirement to get from start to completion* and stripping away everything else that is not critical to the minimum requirement.

- The *resources in the department are valuable* and would not be there if they weren't skilled and needed; it just needs to be determined where they are best utilized.

- *Making adjustments to optimize resources* both reduces waste in poor resource allocation and improves process efficiency by utilizing the best skill sets, making this a power tool for the manager.

- *Evaluating how many resources are used* on which projects ensures that projects are covered and skill sets are assigned correctly to maximize efficiency.

- One tool to evaluate spending is to construct a *Supplier Analysis Matrix.* A supplier analysis looks at both what has to be purchased in the organization and who the qualified suppliers are.

- Managers can mitigate this "perception" by *simply communicating* what meetings they "have" to attend and what their part might be. In setting this type of precedent, the *manager is more transparent and the staff might be more understanding* of the manager's plight with meetings.

- To help eliminate waste, a *decision-making process should be developed* to efficiently guide you through a decision.

- In designing in sustainable change in cost reduction, the manager might find that he can *eliminate a process or combine a process* with another, allowing for a reduction in staff. This not only *eliminates waste,* but *creates positive sustainable change.*

5

Managing Your Resources

Knowing your Resources

Resources make up the backbone of an organization, from human resources to facilities, cash flow and lines of credit, equipment, patents, proprietary and intellectual knowledge—all have to be selected carefully to ensure their value to the organization. Resources are what the organization uses to structure the operation and complete its strategic business objective. Managers are responsible for overseeing processes being performed within the operation that use resources, so how effectively they select and manage resources plays a critical role in the success of the organization.

Resources can vary greatly depending on the organization, how it's structured, and the approach executive management wants to take in designing the organization. Some organizations like service companies are very human resource oriented, whereas others like manufacturing and construction might be more equipment or facility intensive. Managers have to allocate the right resources in a timely and effective manner to accomplish their objective. This chapter covers the tools managers can use in managing several types of resources, including a primary one, human resources.

Human resources is part of every organization at some level, because people create the organization, manage it, and perform tasks and processes associated with it. There are some companies that are more automated and require few human resources to perform tasks, but generally there will be at least one human that started the organization. Human resources, in some ways, are similar to other resources like equipment, machines, and software in that they serve a particular purpose or perform a specific task, but they do have unique attributes that make selecting and managing them a little more interesting and challenging.

Human resources can be one of the hardest types of resources to manage because there are many variables to consider. All types of resources share some common attributes such as these:

1. Qualification for the task
2. Availability
3. Cost
4. Reliability
5. Permanent or temporary state

Many types of resources share these attributes because they are primary to acquiring a resource. Areas such as availability, cost, and permanent or temporary state will be easier to assess because they are more absolute forms of information. Attributes such as qualification and reliability might not be as easy to ascertain because it can be difficult to quantify these for any type of resource if a specific resource has not been used before. This might require some research in refining the type of resource needed or might involve gathering information from references who have used that type of resource to better understand its use and reliability. These attributes are considered more fundamental and not subject to change without notice in most cases, given most types of resources.

In the case of reliability, equipment and machines can break down but this can usually be associated with poor maintenance or just an unforeseen incident that resulted in a failure. Selecting resources that are acceptable in performance and reliability and with proper maintenance should result in the outcome desired. One type of resource that doesn't always fall into this category, because any number of influences can change the performance and reliability, is the human resource. This type of resource has the potential to vary in several different areas as a result of thought processing and mind-set, which other types of resources will not have.

All resources have to be evaluated as to the ability to perform the task required. Usually this information is available when the resource is being acquired and is fairly accurate with little change or variation. Human resource ability will be more difficult to evaluate because the initial information can be rather subjective and might require further evaluation for specific abilities and performance. Given the more subjective nature of human resources, even with in-depth evaluations, the full knowledge of a resource's ability will not be realized until the resource is used in the organization.

Warning

Resource evaluations can result in either positive or negative outcomes based on the level and quality of initial evaluations. Human resources will also have other things to contend with such as attitude, opinions, point of view, and various levels of experience that will shape how the resource makes decisions in his job, much of which will not be realized until after resource is hired.

Human Resources

Operations are conducted primarily by human resources and these resources will need to be acquired in some way. Managers are hired to oversee processes conducted in their department to accomplish the goal of that department. Managers must then understand the skills and experience human resources will need to carry out each process. During the hiring process, managers can have difficulty organizing what they need to do to effectively evaluate potential candidates for a position. The first step in managing human resources is knowing what kinds of skills the resources will need and how to select resources for positions. As with many other areas of managing, hiring human resources simply requires a process.

What Happened to the Great New Hire?

One of the problems managers have to face with the interviewing process is that there will be only so much you can test and evaluate individuals on before they are hired. This leaves learning the rest of who they are, what they know, and how they act until after they are hired. This is where the positive or negative outcomes part comes in because you don't really know these people until they are there working and people can interact with them. As many managers know, there are some who end up being better than anticipated, whereas others fall short of the expectation for whatever reason. Interesting enough, this is usually split between insufficient skills and poor fit in attitude or personality. Skills can be more objectively assessed before hiring, but attitude and personality are usually the surprise after the fact.

It's important to understand that people have different needs and personal situations that can influence how they act on the job. Managing human resources is about understanding them, knowing what makes them tick, and knowing that they are not equal. People have different temperaments and respond to different motivational stimulation.

Power Tool

The important thing here is to make sure that the *resources have proven that they possess the skills required* and have an attitude that will work not only with the manager but also with the rest of the department (team).

The job of the manager will be to refine how the manager deals with all the individuals in the department. The department working as a team is the best environment, and this will largely be a result of the mind-set of the individuals.

Human Resource Skill Set and Utilization

Power Tool

Use only the resources and skill sets that are absolutely needed in your department; *skill set and organization are the key*!

It is very important, in the initial evaluation of potential human resources, to look at both depth and breadth of skills because this is the highest value point the resource can bring. With projects, human resources perform one specific task (skill) or several tasks utilizing a broad base of skills and are allocated based on availability. Having resources with a wide range of skills allows management to better plan resource allocation within the department and organization. This puts more emphasis on the evaluation process, when hiring, to better understand potential resources. Because most managers do understand this importance, the goal here is to connect the value of the skill set to Stream Line Thinking and resource utilization.

The department is at its best when a smaller staff of highly skilled resources is well organized and skills are used at their optimum for highest efficiency. The problem becomes slightly more complex because there are not always highly skilled resources available, and if there are, there might be other issues the manager will need to contend with. There are two sides of the coin when the manager has to evaluate utilization of human resources:

1. What processes to assign highly skilled resources
2. Burnout from overallocation of individual resources

Highly skilled resources are valuable in the department, and the manager must use care in the assignments given because they should be used most efficiently. Problems can surface in overallocating resources, who might become burned out on a process or develop "task resentment." There actually is a threshold of how much extra work a resource can sustain, and this threshold is different for each employee. Resources can feel so strongly against an assignment that they resent being there, and might question the work environment and whether they want to continue being employed. The manager must monitor all resources to ensure that they not only are skilled for a process but also enjoy doing the work.

Human resources do have a gauge in how they feel about their work and general employment with an organization, and that is job satisfaction. Human resources are typically excited about starting a new job and doing the assignments they were hired for. As they become comfortable in their job, they build confidence and draw satisfaction in what they are contributing. Resources, in most cases, don't mind extra tasks now and then, or even temporary reassignments, but this is balanced with knowing that they will go back to their normal job. The manager must be careful in the assignments given to the resources to balance using them effectively and efficiently, and avoid spreading them too thin in assignments producing burnout on tasks that are not part of their normal job.

Resource Mind-Set

When we talk about "mind-set," we are looking at a combination of several things, including attitude, personality, perception, and general buy-in to management and the organization. How managers view their resources is important, and what approach they take in managing their resources is equally important. The manager can have direct input into some areas such as skills and attitude and can require the resource to change or make improvements. Other areas

such as personality, perceptions, and buy-in to management are difficult because managers can't ask resources to change their personality.
Managers can affect perception and buy-in because the manager's
actions can influence those. The mind-set has much to do with the
behaviors that the resources will display and how they interact with
other employees.

In monitoring the resources, the manager needs to assess the general feeling of the department, and understanding the mind-set of
the employees will help the manager better understand attitudes and
behaviors. Having open lines of communication allows the manager to
understand what the resources are feeling and helps in her approach
to managing resources. Because communication is very important in
human resource management, there is a chapter in this text devoted
to that topic.

Power Tool

In projects, the project manager is the hub of all information and
needs to *design and maintain a good communication structure* because this is how the manager will know the details of each segment of the project.

This is also how the project manager can better understand
how human resources on the project are feeling. Maintaining good
communication is a sign of good management and good leadership.
Communication is fundamental in the manager's monitoring and
understanding of his department and the employees he has.

Managing Versus Leading

Managers can have a tendency to be overpowering or to be perceived as a powerful person, which can have a detrimental effect on
human resources. Managers do have a responsibility to oversee and

direct the resources under them, but how this plays out can vary. It is important here to differentiate between "managing" and "leading." Managers have a responsibility to *"manage"* the actions being carried out under their direction to accomplish the processes required by that department. How managers interact or *"lead"* their subordinates in carrying out their tasks is equally important. Under "managing," the resources need to be instructed on the tasks they are to perform, be given the things required to accomplish the tasks, and be held accountable for completing the tasks as scheduled. "Leading" is sometimes seen as the peripheral things that are more the human element of managing. Employees need to know that the manager is listening to them, cares about what they think, and is supportive of them as a resource in the department.

Power Tool

Managers can lead "by example"; this *communicates the attitudes, behaviors, and actions* the manager would like to see in the employees.

This is also how management communicates the importance of various things being done in the organization, by showing that they believe in what the organization is doing.

Management might not always believe in or share the importance of tasks being done in a department, and the resources in the department will feel that and will not be interested in the task. Managers come out of meetings and pick tasks or special projects that they really want to complete while pushing others to the bottom of the priority list. It's very obvious how the manager feels about things that need to be completed based on their attitude and actions. Managers can either gain or lose power in the success of completion largely based on their mind-set. If they believe in a task, their team will believe in it; if they don't, the team will see that and will feel the same way. Success in the completion of tasks is dependent on managers' buy-in and feelings about those tasks' importance in the organization because that is what will be communicated to their department staff.

Allocation of Resources

Project management has an important area to monitor and maintain for efficiency and that is resource organization. How does this differ in managing a functional department? The project will have resources allocated for a short period of time or a fixed amount of time, and after the task is complete they are off of the project and are reassigned elsewhere within the organization. The difference is that resources within a functional group are assigned daily repeated tasks for a longer duration. The allocation of resources should be planned and continually evaluated much like a project.

Power Tool

Project managers control projects by *manipulating resource assignments,* shifting schedules slightly, and maybe bringing in more resources or outsourcing resources that present several different approaches for the manager.

As mentioned earlier, the manager needs to pay close attention to overallocation of resources. Overallocation simply means that the resources are working beyond the normal schedule of work. Either they have more tasks than they can complete in their day or a single task takes them beyond the number of hours scheduled for a day. Overallocated resources might be acceptable for a short period in order to complete a specific task, but this again is not sustainable and is not advisable for long periods.

One technique might be to bring in another resource to take on some of the workload or better distribute the workload over other resources. It might be possible to schedule tasks in parallel to complete tasks more quickly to free up resources. Another technique might be to schedule more time for the work to be completed, but if a large amount of work needs to be completed in a short period, schedule multiple shifts temporarily to complete tasks.

New Managers

Another area of resource allocation and efficiency in the organization is where leads, supervisors, and managers come from. These resources move up through the ranks and are promoted into these positions because they might be the obvious experts within a department. This should be seen as a form of resource allocation because they were assigned tasks in the department and now are simply assigned another task. It would make the most sense to move these resources up in the department so that other resources see them as a leadership role and ask questions and get mentoring and guidance in doing their work.

Some organizations like to hire their managers from outside to give more of an objective perspective of their group, so a tip here would be to carefully select supervisory and manager-level positions, determining who is moved up and who is brought in. If we take a key, experienced individual and promote him to a supervisor or manager, he will no longer be performing the role he was doing, leaving a void to fill. This resource was an expert in his role, and management has now taken that skill set out of the direct process, which might not be in the best interest of the department. Other cases might allow for a natural leader to emerge and take on more responsibility. This is where cross-training can result in other resources stepping in to cover for the loss in experience.

Some resources can lead people and mentor through good training, communication skills, and working well with others, whereas others, though experts, might not have these skills. Managing and leading are another whole set of skills that have to be evaluated in resources moving up because not everyone is cut out to lead. Management is looking at ways they can make an operation more efficient by simplifying. This will force us to evaluate our management structure to ensure that we have the proper amount of management oversight and processes are staffed correctly.

Capital Equipment

The second primary area of resources in the organization is capital equipment. There is a tendency to put more attention on human resources when we consider efficiency in streamlining the organization, and many times capital equipment use and facility space utilization are overlooked. This is also an area where equipment, much like human resources, needs to be used effectively and efficiently. When human resources are not being used, it is usually more obvious, and actions can be taken to use or eliminate them. If equipment or space in the facility is not being used, or is being inefficiently used, it is easy to not see it and ignore it. This starts with reminding ourselves what capital equipment might be.

Capital equipment can be in the form of office equipment and furniture, manufacturing machines, forklifts, trucks, and even shelving and pallet racking, as well as buildings and generally everything needed to run the organization. We also have to consider why we have these items, whether they are being used now, whether they will be used in the future, and how much space will be needed to house the equipment. Evaluating the size of the building requires many things to be evaluated, such as total capital equipment needed, office space, any manufacturing, and inventory, as well as shipping and receiving.

Power Tool

The key to managing capital equipment resources falls into two areas: *the utilization of capital equipment* and *the reallocation of resources if something changes.*

Operations management typically defines the utilization of resources based on the business strategy. In project management the utilization of resources is by design in the project based on the tasks that need to be completed or in reallocation of resources as necessary if something changes or goes wrong. It is not that much different in operations management; there is a defined strategic objective of the organization which should produce requirements that the organization will need in order to fulfill completion of that goal. In operations we consider two primary areas: facilities and capital equipment.

Facilities

Most organizations utilize some form of building structure to house the operation. This can be in the form of a space located within a residence, all the way to large factories and office buildings scattered around the world. In structuring the operations, executive management has made decisions as to what facilities will be required to achieve the business objective. This usually involves the size of the buildings, type of buildings, and location of buildings. After facilities have been acquired, tenant improvements will be made to create office space, production floors, inventory control, shipping and receiving, break rooms, and restrooms, and at that point the operation is usually underway. The operations manager has to monitor the use of the facility and/or the space used for their department in the facility for optimal use of space.

When the organization first moves into a facility, it is easy to utilize all the space even if it's more than required. This might be a result of moving from a smaller facility to a larger facility or having worked in restricted workspaces and now having more room to spread out. This is okay if it was by design, but care must be taken because square footage is expensive and a justification for space needs to be closely watched by those setting up the new facility.

Power Tool

One area in which the manager can be effective is in being *conservative with the allocation of space* within the department and *planning for future growth.*

This is Streamline Thinking—preparing for future growth and not placing that burden for space on the organization at a later date. This gives the manager some latitude in control over what's happening within the department because things usually will come up that require more space.

Project managers are taught and trained not only to manage and control their project, but also to be watching for risk events that are identified as having a probability of occurring. Part of risk planning involves having a contingency plan in place in the event that a risk event ever occurs. Managers should view their department in much the same way, and the use of facility space might fall under this category.

Power Tool

If the manager has *designed areas in the facility for unplanned use,* this would allow the manager to alter something within the department and utilize extra space without creating an extra burden on the organization and facility.

These extra spaces might not have to be very big, and would be designed as contingency space if needed. This might also include space swapping within the organization.

Space swapping is another project management tool used in operations that allows for the most optimum use of space within a facility. Some departments might have space available for other departments to use or might have the ability to swap things going on in their department with another department for a better utilization of space. This might be as a result of a layout constriction that presents a problem for one department but can be used very well by another department, in which case space swapping allows more efficient use of the facility space. Space swapping can also come in handy for emergency use of extra space needed within a department. This is another tool used in project management to overcome problems that will slow down a project.

Power Tool

Managers can review the space in their department and *space swap with other managers* if a particular project or task underway in their department is using too much space. This allows for a more *optimum use of space in the facility.*

Equipment

The second area in capital equipment involves all the equipment, tools, heavy equipment machines, computers, and office equipment. Because managers are responsible for their department with human resources and facility space utilization, they also have equipment of some kind that will be issued for the purpose of their department. Organizations can look at the acquisition of capital equipment in two ways: purchase of equipment or lease of equipment.

Depending on what the equipment is used for and how long the operation will need the equipment, the organization will have to determine what would be best, purchase of equipment or a short-term lease of equipment. If the lease of equipment is selected as the best plan of action, the manager responsible for that equipment must monitor how long he will actually be using it and whether that time-frame needs to be extended or shortened. This is where the manager can benefit the organization by not allowing lease equipment to sit unused in a department for extended periods of time, costing the organization unnecessary expense (waste). In other cases the short-term lease is best choice to acquire equipment to accomplish a task or process and not place the burden of purchasing that equipment if it is not needed long-term in the operation.

Power Tool

Beware of leased equipment that *sits in the organization too long* and is *wasting money and taking up space.*

Capital equipment such as office equipment, power equipment used in manufacturing, and heavy equipment used in construction needs to be evaluated and selected, much like human resources, as to their need in the organization and as to whether that piece of equipment is sufficient to meet that need. Streamline Thinking should have the managers reviewing the equipment used in their department to ensure that it is adequate for the process required and is actually being used and not stored long-term. This can impose unneeded stress within the organization on both unutilized capital equipment and storing this equipment within the facility in space that can be used for something else.

Power Tool

Have only the capital *equipment needed in order to perform the processes required by the department* because all else will be an added cost and storage burden on the organization.

The selection, justification, and utilization of human resources, facilities, and capital equipment are important for the manager to monitor and maintain. Proper selection and utilization of these resources can give the manager more confidence in control of the department processes and control of cost overhead for the organization. These are important tools for the manager to be successful in the organization.

Power Tools Summary

- The important thing here is to make sure the *resources have proven that they possess the skills required* and have an attitude that will work not only with the manager but also with the rest of the department (team).

- Only use the resources and skill sets that are absolutely needed in your department; *skill set and organization are the key!*

- In projects, the project manager is the hub of all information and needs to *design and maintain a good communication structure* because this is how the manager will know the details of each segment of the project.

- Managers can lead "by example"; this *communicates the attitudes, behaviors, and actions* the manager would like to see in the employees.

- Project managers control projects by *manipulating resource assignments,* shifting schedules slightly, maybe bringing in more resources or outsourcing resources that present several different approaches for the manager.

- The key to managing capital equipment resources falls into two areas: *the utilization of capital equipment* and the *reallocation of resources if something changes.*

- One area in which the manager can be effective is in being *conservative with the allocation of space* within the department and *planning for future growth.*

- If the manager has *designed areas in the facility for unplanned use,* this would allow the manager to alter something within the department and utilize extra space without creating an extra burden on the organization and facility.

- Managers can review the space in their department and *space swap with other managers* if a particular project or task underway in their department is using too much space. This allows for a more *optimum use of space in the facility.*

- Beware of leased equipment that *sits in the organization too long* and is *wasting money* and *taking up space.*

- Have only the capital *equipment needed in order to perform the processes required by the department* because all else will be an added cost and storage burden on the organization.

6

Budget Control

Operations are run by the allocation of several types of resources. These can include the use of human resources, capital equipment, facilities, and finances. With the exception of some organizations that are run with volunteer human resources, most organizations require finances to manage the acquisition of resources. The organization having a purpose, called a strategic objective, needs to procure resources to accomplish that objective. Finances in the form of cash, lines of credit, or investor capitol are typically used in purchasing resources, managing an operation, and payment of salaries for human resources. In maintaining the operation, these financial expenditures need to be outlined and organized so that executives in charge of the operation can plan for purchases and expenses needed throughout the year. This detailed assessment of planned purchases and expenses is called a budget.

This plan for expenditures is then distributed throughout the organization to appropriate management put in charge of functional areas participating in these expenditures. The chief financial officer of the organization can choose to break out individual budgets for smaller portions of the operation such as divisions or departments within the organization. These budgets will be more specific to those functional areas and will need to be managed by the manager in charge of those functional areas. Because budgets are an outline of purchases and expenditures within a functional area, how these budgets are derived and how accurate they are to actual spending is vital in planning adequate financial resources for the organization. Emphasis should be placed on correctly establishing a budget and controlling the budget throughout the year because this will help ensure the proper management of financial resources.

When you are looking at the ability to control a budget, part of the general feeling of control is having ownership or knowing that you had a part in designing or developing what it is you are trying to control. One aspect of looking into budgets and control of a budget is how rigid the budget is and how firmly the manager has to stay on that budget. A budget might simply be a cost-structuring guideline that allows the manager to get a feel for what's going to be purchased for general expenditures in the department or on a particular project. If this is the case, a guideline is something you try to shoot for, and it will give upper management an idea of how to cost-structure next quarter's or next year's budget based on the outcome of the previous year. Although this works as a budget-estimating tool, this typically is not the way upper management would like to view the managing of a "controllable" budget. Managers need to hold to a budget and try to manage any cost overruns, and this is where the problems start—in how to *control* a budget!

Establishing a Budget

Budgets are created based on data from each department or division about what is required to run that part of the operation. Each organization establishes how it creates budgets and how it will be managed. The information required in creating a budget might or might not be available to the immediate manager; therefore, the manager might not always get to develop her own budget. Budgets can be developed two ways:

- **Top-down**—Budgets are created by upper management and given to lower-level managers to administer.

- **Bottom-up**—Budgets are created by the lower-level or immediate manager.

When budgets are handed down to managers, the manager has little or no control over the creation of the budget. This is typically more difficult to work with because you simply have to be held to a budgetary number but have little or no control over where the number was derived from and how accurate it's going to be. Budgets developed with the input of the manager might be better to work with, because the manager has generally more detail about the department or division and can give a more objective assessment of what that budget might be.

In some organizations a budget might be based on historical data from budgets used in the past for a given department, or input from other functional managers. This would be considered a hybrid between the manager fully establishing his own budget and the budget being passed down; the manager might have some say in it but will not dictate the overall construction of the budget. In any case, a project or department will have some form of cost structuring that will need to be established based on what is being accomplished within that department or project.

Upper management, when handing down a budget to a manager, will want to see the manager hold to the budget as closely as possible. This in turn gives members of upper management a feel for how well the manager is able to control her project or department, in addition to giving them a feel for whether the person actually has the capability of controlling a budget versus just reporting it. Upper management, with or without help from the manager, has established a budget and wants the manager to stick very rigidly to that budget and can in some cases be reprimanded if the manager steps outside of the budget boundaries. This is especially difficult if the manager did not have much say in developing the budget, but *control of the budget can still be possible* even under these more rigorous requirements.

Power Tool

The manager should strive to *be a part of establishing a budget* because this not only allows the manager to *have more input* with *accurate information,* but also gives the manager a better sense of how the budget will operate and *ownership of the budget* in helping to establish it.

When managers have the ability and are allowed input on developing a budget, they have a tendency to be more proactive about managing the budget and feel a sense of ownership.

This approach is usually preferred by managers because they then have the complete discretionary capability of analyzing most of the details within a department and know they are putting together a much more accurate budget they can actually stick to. Depending on the skill of the manager, budgets can be established poorly because the manager simply is not skilled in how to estimate costs; in other cases the managers does very well and is educated, experienced, and skilled at cost estimating and structuring a budget. This is actually the best way an organization can establish budgets and have managers maintain control over their budgets.

In either case, whether a budget has been passed down from upper management or has been established by the manager, it has to be clearly understood by the manager whether or not the budget has to be strictly followed or is simply a guideline for the manager to stay as close to as possible. This is important when it comes to budget control because there are some controls that can be used to manage a budget, keeping things strictly within its guidelines, whereas other tools simply manage a budget from more of a guideline standpoint.

Scope of the Budget

Managers might have cost and expense management for everything related to a department's operation, including human resources, capital equipment, facilities, and any type of cost requiring cash or lines of credit needed for the department's operation. In some cases the departmental manager might simply have the cost structuring of employee salaries and managing hours, and that might be all. There might be a case in which a manager is in charge of a department with lots of projects running and might or might not have to include everything related to those projects in the budget of that department. It might be that the projects have their own Project Manager and budget associated with them and are not connected to the departmental budget. This type of information is critical to define in establishing and maintaining a budget because the manager needs to know what they are to control and what boundaries are set for the scope of the budget.

Budgeting Subcontractors

Some budgets might have to include the use of contracts set up with subcontractors or contracts established for procurement purposes that happen in the course of the year. These types of arrangements can make cost estimating a budget difficult at the beginning of the year, as well as maintaining the budget throughout the year. If the need to hire subcontractors or rent capital equipment is known at the beginning of the year, a budget for each contract can be estimated, but in many cases these requirements come up with little warning and the added expense is in addition to the budget. There might be times when negotiations of procurements fail and new contracts have to be established with new pricing that goes over budget. Working with contracts in procurements is good because it establishes pricing early and will be guaranteed so that it can be put in the budget. There are tools for dealing with this type of problem that give the manager more control over these situations.

Unforeseen Costs and Risk Budgeting

The department might see changes that happen by surprise due to risk or unforeseen events that happen without any foreknowledge or planning, and these changes might cause overruns on a budget. One of the hardest things to deal with in managing a budget is when problems occur that create added expenditures and it feels as though there is no way to control these events to avoid going over budget. There might have been employees who were terminated or who left the organization, allowing for the human resource part of the budget to decrease. In other cases, more resources might have been brought on due to changes in the business that were not expected, which inflated the budget. How we manage change to a budget is critical, and understanding tools and techniques to incorporate these changes, getting approvals for changes, and managing changes to help stay within an existing budget are important and vital to managing the overall finances of the organization.

Controlling a Budget

It is important to understand that budgets can be very simple or complex depending on what the budget is trying to cover. The focus of this chapter is not on establishing budgets or where budgets come from, but on the control of a budget, because this is generally more difficult to do within a project or department. When looking at control, we have to understand that there are two things that happen when managers are given responsibility over a budget. Managers have to report on the status of their spending, and they are held accountable for the spending within their department.

Managers who simply have to report on budgetary spending find it easy because there are several channels from which they can derive this information. This can be done through status meetings, during which invoicing and reports from procurement, finance, and accounting will show what is happening financially within the department. This unfortunately only gives the manager information about what has already happened, and if spending has gone outside of what the budget was intending, the manager will be held accountable and will need to answer for why the spending is different from what was budgeted. This makes life hard on the manager, and at this point the manager might feel that although he has accurately reported what has happened, he has little or no control over what has happened. He might feel as though he cannot fix, mitigate, or eliminate a problem and therefore has no control. That is why this chapter is focused on establishing tools and techniques to help managers understand that they can control a budget and not simply report on it.

There are five essential areas that have to be considered within the control mechanism that will have to be done in order to successfully control a budget. These five elements of control consist of the following:

1. Estimating a budget to create a baseline
2. Monitoring
3. Measuring
4. Adjusting
5. Verifying

Estimating a Budget

As mentioned earlier, information for estimating the budget can come in two different forms. The first form involves a top-down organizational philosophy in which budgets are derived by upper management and given to managers to be used within their department. This information comes from the upper management structure of establishing this budget and in most cases from historical data, but in some cases from managerial experience. The second form of estimating comes from a bottom-up type of estimating and is generally more accurate and detailed information that comes from within the department itself and is compiled by the manager for use in creating a budget.

Budgetary estimating should be as detailed as possible to allow the manager more opportunity to view specific cost elements within the department or project. The more detail within cost structuring, the more ways a manager can control variations in cost.

Here's another look at the two forms:

- **Top-down**—Estimating typically tends to be more generalized and more compartmentalized in structure, which yields a more "overview" look of what will be spent within the department, but not necessarily having the detail that most managers would like.

- **Bottom-up**—Estimating typically has the capability of more detail, giving the manager the most amount of information about purchases and cost structuring and giving the manager the most amount of leverage in control.

In either case a budget will be established and the manager will need to hold to this budget to some degree. If the manager has the bottom-up estimating capability or cost estimating from within the department, this should be used to its fullest extent. Actual data can come via several sources such as these:

- Actual invoicing
- Prior historical purchases
- Real employee costs
- Subcontractor costs
- Contractual agreements for procurements

There might also be *subject matter experts* available within the department who can give insight as to more accurate cost figures the manager can use. The manager should always strive to look for as much detail, from as many resources, as possible in order to get the most accurate estimates in establishing a budget. There might even be cases in which departmental managers have notes or lessons-learned documents that might give insight into prior problems with purchases, cost estimating, or contracts that were mistakes in the past; these can help the manager avoid making the same mistakes again. This can be valuable information because it can help mitigate or eliminate possible risks within a budget that might result in overspending or having to make purchases based on things that have gone wrong in the past.

This detailed information also sheds light on the possibility of risk items or uncertainties that have the capability of costing a department money, and gives the manager an opportunity to pad a cost estimate that allows a budget to have money in case the risk actually happens. This is an area where managers can estimate a budget that actually allows for uncertainty and risk. When the budget status is reported, it shows on budget even when risks might be occurring if the manager has allowed room for those within the budget. This is an area where a manager has the ability to control a budget and not simply report on a risk happening that will be out of the budget.

Power Tool

Properly cost estimating and budgeting for risk is the first step a manager can take in actually controlling a budget.

It is important to know how accurate budgetary numbers are, as this will indicate how much padding to use in estimating. Some padding might be from known historical problems; other padding might be simply used for protecting from potential risk. It is better to plan for risk and to not have to use the extra budget than it is to not plan for it and end up needing it and going over budget.

Power Tool

When risks are fixed within the budget and the budget can be reported as stable, the manager *feels as though she has more control* over the budget.

If risks were budgeted for but did not happen, this allows the manager to show that he is under budget. Managers might need to be careful with this because in some organizations annual budget approvals are based on how well a manager is able to stay on a budget, which includes going too far over or under.

In some cases budgets might be cut because not enough money has been spent. The manager needs to show that there was cost budgeting factored in based on prior risk events typical within that department. The manager was being responsible in covering risk within the budget. It should also be noted that managers should try to lobby for this type of estimating because it does allow for more accurate budget projections. In most organizations it's better to come in under budget than over. What's also valuable for the manager is to show that the manager not only is responsible in paying attention to detail, but also has a plan for how to deal with risk.

Establishing a Baseline

One of the most important tools a manager needs in understanding how to control a budget is to have a way to measure what is actually happening against what was planned. The first step is to accurately estimate costs that will be used to establish the budget. After a budget has been estimated, another area within cost estimating is to use the initial estimate as a baseline. The baseline is simply the starting point at which the budget has been established; all the cost items have been listed but nothing has actually been purchased yet.

Power Tool

The baseline is a very important tool the manager can use *to track the success of control efforts* as *measured against the original estimate.*

This is why the baseline is vitally important—it gives the manager a way to monitor department spending and measure it to see how things are going. Project managers have used the baseline tool for decades as a primary weapon to control project costs. The manager can better assess what controls are needed based on how far or close the actual spending is to the original baseline estimate. When the budget is monitored and measured on a continual basis, this allows a real-time assessment of budgetary spending and gives the manager the quickest indication as to trends in spending and potential problem areas that might need to have adjustments made.

Some organizations set an annual budget of operating expenses for departments at the beginning of the year. One might ask whether changes are allowed within the budget if it was used to establish a baseline and will be used throughout the entire year; the answer should be yes. If the answer is no, meaning that changes cannot be made in the budget throughout the year, the manager will need to have other control tools in place to keep departmental spending on budget. If the organization can allow changes throughout the year, this might allow for the budget to be updated and the manager would be allowed to change the baseline to reflect those changes.

Warning

The organization allowing changes to a budget should not be used to reset the baseline based on cost overruns because this gives a false impression of the performance of actual spending compared to the original budget. Adjustments to the baseline should be done *only* when permanent changes in areas such as staffing or capital equipment are made that make a big impact on the budget and cannot be controlled to maintain the baseline.

One of the best tools a manager can have in understanding when and how to control the budget is the baseline. The fewer changes to the baseline the better, because it is supposed to represent an accurate picture of planned spending to be used to compare to actual real-time spending. Maintaining the integrity of the baseline will ensure that controlling efforts are actually justified and show how much control really needs to be implemented. Using the baseline tool helps the manager control costs and saves the organization money in staying on budget.

Monitoring

After the budget has been estimated and the baseline has been set, the baseline needs to be used to compare actual to planned spending, which will require a monitoring system established to gather data on the actual spending. This is important because the manager will not know whether changes need to be made or controls need to be implemented, if no attention is being paid to what is actually being purchased. Managers are responsible for many things, including the oversight of a budget. As stressed at the beginning of this chapter, oversight of a budget is not simply reporting on what is happening, but actually controlling departmental spending.

After a budget is in place, the department manager must have tools to monitor the purchases, expenses, and salaries of employees happening real-time. This is important because this information will be compared against the baseline to see whether changes or adjustments need to be made to stay within the budget. The manager must know the budget well enough to know what information for purchases, expenses, and salaries will need to be obtained and where to retrieve it. Monitoring can be in the form of status meetings, having e-mail updates daily or weekly, or physically going to the areas where procurements and expenses are actually happening to get this information as it becomes available.

Power Tool

The manager must *set up a regularly scheduled flow of real-time budget information* to compare to the baseline; this gives the manager the quickest indication of problems and the *fastest response time in addressing issues.*

Monitoring will look at two directions of the spending path:

1. Monitoring procurements and expenses that are in process or have already occurred

2. Monitoring the schedule for future planned spending to ensure that it will be done as planned and look for any planned risks or potential problems that might be approaching

In monitoring spending that is currently in play or has already happened, assessments are made as to whether spending is still on budget or damage control needs to be implemented. This might require adjustments or changes in immediate procurements to control any further problems and/or controls for further spending to avoid problems.

Power Tool

Monitoring will also be directed to future planned spending to see whether problems might be imminent or whether risks that have been identified need to be addressed. This level of monitoring is very important because it allows the baseline to be used in mitigation of problems, *which is proactive versus reactive managing.*

Measuring

In the course of monitoring, the manager will discover all the areas of spending where data will need to be collected. When real-time data is being gathered on a regular basis, there are two things this data can be used for:

1. Documenting actual procurements and expenses
2. Comparing actual data to the baseline to see whether adjustments need to be made and reporting the status of budgetary spending to upper management

Measuring actual spending compared to the baseline data can reveal how much control will be required, if any. The primary tool used in measuring is the *comparison to the baseline data.* Depending on the complexity and structuring of a department, some items might need more monitoring and measuring because variability can change without notice and very quickly. Other items might not be as subject to change or might not occur as frequently, so monitoring and measuring will be in place relative to the frequency of occurrence. As with cost estimating, measuring of real-time data needs to be as accurate as the baseline to make valid comparisons.

If cost estimates were detailed and actual cost measurements were very broad, this would not give you a very accurate comparison to your baseline. Measuring accuracy should match the level of accuracy in the original estimates and baseline. When you are gathering information, care must be taken if you are using second- and third-hand information because this can also be an area of risk and can result in inaccurate reporting of real-time information. When gathering real-time information about individual cost items, make sure that it includes everything the original cost element included. For instance, if the original cost estimate of an item included delivery charges, sales tax, or special conditions, evaluate the procured item to see what was "actually" charged. It is imperative that the manager try to get *firsthand information* and the *most accurate information* possible so that this can be used in comparison to the original estimate or baseline to more accurately gauge how well spending is performing in the budget.

Adjusting

A vital component in controlling a budget is being able to make adjustments to bring overbudgeted areas back in line. Some managers might think controlling a budget involves simply approving purchases, and although this is one component of control, there are other forms of control that can be more effective. If, in the course of monitoring and measuring expenses and procurements, you see a major problem starting to occur, adjustments should be made to bring expenditures back closer to the original estimate or the baseline. This is the action component of control; it is where you've not only measured what is going out of budget, but also measured how far it's gone out. You'll need to take action to bring this item closer if it's not within the baseline.

Techniques to control costs within an operation include these:

1. **Evaluate pricing**—Consider best pricing versus a qualified vendor list. Depending on how rigid the organization is on qualifying vendors, there might be better pricing from nonqualified vendors who simply need to be qualified. This can be a much more difficult process with organizations that have a very strict qualifying process. It doesn't hurt to ask!

2. **Verify specifications required**—Make sure that those who are purchasing understand what they are purchasing so that specifications, requirements, and the scope of the purchase are made correctly. If little attention is paid to the details, this can present problems when items arrive and do not meet the requirements. This requires returns and more delays, all costing time, resources, and money.

3. **Know who is authorized to purchase**—If critical purchases need to be made, ensure that those making the purchases are trained and qualified to do so. Some purchases might require special negotiation or contractual agreements. Others might simply require knowing where to go for best pricing or shipping requirements.

4. **Make or buy**—Knowing when to use internal versus external resources to accomplish a procured item is very important. The externally purchased item is typically thought to be more expensive, but only if there are internal resources capable of making it cheaper, faster, and with equal quality. In some cases those internal resources are not available and external purchases are necessary. When internal resources are used that are not as capable, it might be more expensive given the time, lack of tools, and lack of experience, as well as any rework it took to complete something. This can also apply to using subcontractors to perform processes. Process demand and resource allocation will determine whether internal or external staff will be chosen to fulfill that need.

Making adjustments is about doing what it takes to address the cost element of something that has gone over budget. When we focus on what drives the cost of something, this can take us into other areas of indirect or periphery influence of cost and surprising ways you might make adjustments. With this type of adjusting, the manager needs to think out-of-the-box in being creative and understanding the item that has gone over budget. This also requires understanding the things surrounding the item that can have an influence on cost to which adjustments can be made, bringing the cost closer to the baseline.

Looking beyond the simple cost of something should have the manager asking questions like these:

- Are all the specific requirements listed that drive a cost *actually* needed?

- Can you benefit from using a vendor that, based on location, will result in less expensive freight charges, or from shopping vendors that have free shipping available based on the types of purchases?

- Can setting up scheduled releases of shipments allow for volume pricing based on larger purchase quantities, but establishes controlled delivery?

When evaluating the number and types of human resources required, the manager should pay close attention to the complexity of the process and skill sets required to perform the process. Human resources with a marginal skill set might take longer to perform a task and in the long run might cost more money than a more skilled and experienced resource who could do it in a shorter period and possibly with higher quality. This type of assessment of human resources should always be taken into consideration to streamline the efficiency of the department, as well as completing the processes required. Having an expensive, highly skilled resource allocated to a process might be overkill if a lesser skilled person can do the process just fine but at a lower cost.

The manager should also monitor the use of contractors and how contracts might be set up. Hiring a subcontractor to do a portion of work within the department might have a contract cost associated with a particular level of work, but that contract could be renegotiated to alter some component of work or possibly a different contractor could do the work for less money. The contractor might be working with resources in the department who were pulled away from their tasks, indirectly costing the department more money because of resources having to help the contractor.

When looking at the budget and monitoring what has to be purchased, managers can look into the details of purchases, ask the questions before things get purchased, and try to be ahead of purchasing to make adjustments if there is an opportunity. Just asking the questions puts visibility on purchases and accountability on those requesting the purchases before they are made to avoid overspending. This also gives the manager more control over spending and the budget. This might not result in any lower costs of items, but it ensures that the procurements and expenses happening within the department are justified and represent the most cost-effective option.

This is why monitoring and measuring are vital tools managers need to have in place to better understand how they can truly control the budget. When these tools are in place, managers have the information they need to look ahead and make accurate assessments as to the procurements, contracts, and human resource allocation that will actually fall in line with the objectives of the department, as well as matching the estimates laid out in the budget for that department. Managers feel much better about their level of control when they can make adjustments before things happen and can see the outcome of their action staying on budget.

Verifying

The next and final area is that of verifying the adjustments and validating whether they've actually completed or accomplished the goal. Verifying, although seemingly unnecessary, is actually very important because this is where the manager really understands the outcome or effect the adjustment has made on the budget. Much like monitoring and measuring, in which the manager was able to verify costs in the budget against the baseline, verifying does the same thing in making sure that adjustments actually resulted in the expected outcome. It's important for managers to verify their adjustments for the following reasons:

1. The manager can see how much adjustment was actually made and whether it was successful in accomplishing what the manager was trying to do in lowering costs.

2. The manager is assured that his strategy of making adjustments actually does work.

3. The manager will see that an adjustment affected only what was intended to reduce cost and did not cause other ripple effect problems elsewhere within the budget.

This is very important as managers begin to understand how they can make adjustments and become comfortable in being able to proactively or reactively start controlling their budget. Verifying adjustments gives direct feedback to the manager that adjustments were actually made and they can realize a cost savings that actually happened. Verification can also be a necessary tool that will help the manager to explain how adjustments were made, and for what reasons, and to show a level of competency in being able to control budgets.

Contracts

Contracts are used throughout the organization for several reasons. Contracts can be used in hiring human resources permanently or temporarily. They can be used with vendors to establish agreements on certain procurements or with subcontractors for services provided. Contracts are typically regarded as legal and binding, so they must be written by people who know the different types of contracts, details, and restrictions in contractual legal documents. Although there is a serious legal aspect, contracts can be great tools for establishing and guaranteeing products, services, pricing, and balancing risk.

There are various types of contracts, but the most common are fixed-price contracts. This is where both parties agree on the deliverable and the price will not change. This puts most of the risk on the party producing the deliverable for the price agreed on in the contract.

Power Tool

Contracts can *benefit the manager* in not only estimating but controlling budget items because contractual *pricing should not change or be influenced.*

The drawback is the rigid nature of contracts and the inability for managers to make necessary adjustments to control the budget. One primary concern is in the ability to terminate a contract if needed. Both parties must be convinced that in agreeing to the terms of the contract, it's in their best interest *before* they sign. After the contract is signed, the primary way out of the contract is with a breach of contract. This is where one party does not fulfill his part of the contract and the other party can request a termination of contract.

Managers must know that they cannot simply turn on and off contracts at will if the terms are not suitable—these are legally binding agreements! If there are contracts relative to subcontractors, equipment lease/rentals, or procurement of material required within the budget, the manager should pay very close attention to those items because after contracts are signed, although some things can be changed through a change process, they are very difficult to cancel.

When controlling or making adjustments, the manager could look at altering the conditions of the contract through a *change process* to see whether lowering the cost within the existing agreement is possible. This could be as a result of learning that the deliverable could change or supplies and materials might be found at a much lower price and a new contracted price could be agreed on. Because making changes to an existing contract might or might not be possible, the manager can use this information to look forward to future procurements. The manager can evaluate purchases that have not been made and possibly streamline through cuts within the budget to make room for overcost on items already purchased. This is another critical tool that managers can use to again control a budget. Control is about making changes and adjustments that allow the budget to stay on its original estimated values. If changes cannot be made to things already purchased or bound by contract, then changes can be made to things that have not yet been purchased. This again has the manager thinking out-of-the-box and looking at his entire budget for areas of adjustment.

Evaluating past expenditures to identify problems and then looking ahead on the budget is another proactive way to help streamline certain procurements or reevaluate contracts or agreements. Contracts can also be used in making adjustments in the budget by shifting a make-or-buy decision which allows for a task or an item to actually come in less expensive. This is an interesting area for organizations to evaluate because many organizations find themselves in a situation in which they do not have resources or material to do something in-house and have to contract or buy from outside the organization to fulfill that need.

In other cases organizations have human resources, materials, or equipment available to perform tasks in-house at lower costs, not needing to go outside the organization to fulfill those requirements. The manager looking ahead on her budget has the ability to assess or analyze a make-or-buy situation that might help improve the budget. This will also have the manager evaluating resource capability versus availability. In evaluating cost reduction, it might be less expensive to do things internally, whereas in other cases it might be less expensive to go outside. A thorough analysis should be done in either case to see how improvements can be made to the budget regarding these types of procurements and the need for contracts.

Conclusion

As you have seen, managers have a responsibility within a department to understand how a budget was made, whether they were a part of establishing the budget or not, and how to put into place a monitoring system in which they can see areas of the budget that are happening. The manager also knows the importance of establishing a reference or baseline of the budget as a tool to measure and compare actual performance against. The manager then needs to monitor and gather actual data on expenses, procurements, and contracts to measure against that baseline to see whether spending is within the budget or control needs to take place in order to get costs back within budget. Based on evaluation of the real data compared to the budget plan, the manager can make adjustments from one of two different perspectives:

- **In the reactive mode**—The manager makes adjustments real-time or looks at what *was* purchased to see whether anything can be renegotiated, stopped, or repurchased to fix an overbudget area. This is more of a damage-control approach.

- **In the proactive mode**—The manager looks forward within the budget and analyzes whether things could be done slightly better or could be done at less cost. This gives the manager more power and leverage in control because things have not happened yet and changes can be made to avoid problems or simply make better choices. This is more of a damage-avoidance approach.

In either case, the manager knows that he has the tools to not only develop the budget, but also to monitor and analyze spending to ensure that he stays on budget.

Power Tool

Knowing that budgets can be controlled gives the manager *a sense of ownership* and *power over spending* in not just reporting budget outcomes, but trying to *control spending to stay on budget.*

These five areas—establishing a budget, monitoring, measuring, adjusting, and verifying—are all part of controlling a budget and are some of the most powerful tools the manager can have with regard to departmental budgets.

Power Tool Summary

- The manager should strive to *be a part of establishing a budget* because this not only allows the manager to *have more input* with *accurate information,* but also gives the manager a better sense of how the budget will operate and *ownership of the budget* in helping to establish it.
- *Properly cost estimating and budgeting for risk* is the first step a manager can take in actually controlling a budget.
- When risks are fixed within the budget and the budget can be reported as stable, the manager *feels as though she has more control* over the budget.
- The baseline is a very important tool the manager can use *to track the success of control efforts measured against the original estimate.*
- The manager must *set up a regularly scheduled flow of real-time budget information* to compare to the baseline; this gives the manager the quickest indication of problems and the *fastest response time in addressing issues.*
- Monitoring will also be directed to future planned spending to see whether problems might be imminent or whether risks that have been identified need to be addressed. This level of monitoring is very important because it allows the baseline to be used in mitigation of problems, *which is proactive versus reactive managing.*

- Contracts can *benefit the manager* in not only estimating but controlling budget items as contractual *pricing should not change or be influenced.*
- Knowing that budgets can be controlled gives the manager *a sense of ownership* and *power over spending* in not just reporting budget outcomes, but trying to *control spending to stay on budget.*

7

Don't Be Afraid of Risks

Risk in Today's Operations

Operations managers are faced with many challenges that require the manager to either plan or respond to situations. This can include planning for regular processes conducted within the department, planning for special projects, and planning for new items the department will undertake. One area managers might struggle with is in dealing with problems that could arise from any number of different sources. This can be a difficult area for management to train and prepare for because problems can be unpredictable and solutions can vary depending on the size and complexity of the problems.

Although problems are inevitable, managers should not be afraid of problems simply because of their elusive nature. Managers typically do not like problems for two primary reasons: the resulting damage to cost, schedule, or quality, and the response or lack of response planning to deal with the problem and what that will require. When a problem occurs, the manager now has more work in damage control, which adds to an already hectic workload. In looking at problems, a primary issue is the fact that they are simply not planned and this is why problems can create stress for the manager.

Project managers have the same responsibility in overseeing a project because problems can occur, but there are tools they can use to plan for risk and how to respond to problems. Project managers also make this the culture of the project so that everyone is aware of the tools and techniques to plan and address problems.

Lost Opportunity

Organizations are formulated primarily in response to an opportunity to provide a product or service within a particular market. It's interesting how the very nature of creating an organization presents risk and potential failure. This did not stop the founders of the organization from taking risk when they invested in the creation and development of the organization. In some cases, acting in response to a problem presented an opportunity that an organization could capitalize on, resulting in a new product or service, or simply more efficiency within the operation. It's this same mind-set that managers need to take in approaching their responsibilities. Problems can present opportunities for new things, as well as an opportunity to improve current areas within their responsibility.

Throughout history, organizations at many levels have capitalized on problems, resulting in bigger and better things for the organization. This might involve new product introductions, a failed attempt in an engineering lab that resulted in a new way to do something and possibly a patent, or a problem revealing a hidden element of the business that can now be improved. One thing is for sure: When problems occur it is how management responds to problems that reveals the maturity, professionalism, and experience the organization has in dealing with problems.

Power Tool

When managers are *trained and educated* and *know how to identify and plan for problems,* they can operate in a *proactive mode rather than a reactive mode.*

Proactive Versus Reactive

Having the responsibility of managing an operation or a department requires, among several other things, the knowledge and skill of planning. Planning, by definition, is a proactive approach to identifying tasks and scheduling. When managers are responsible for various processes, they first have to identify what's required in the process, and then schedule the tasks within the processes. This can include human resources, capital equipment, office or warehouse space, manufacturing resources, or anything else required in carrying out the process. After the identification of resources is complete, scheduling of these resources will be required to complete the process. This is the primary function of a manager—identifying, planning, and scheduling, and having a clear understanding of the objective, is what managers are used to doing as a part of their responsibility. This is a proactive approach to their responsibility; they have identified what has to be done and have developed a plan to carry out those actions. If problems can be identified early on, and a response plan can be developed with a desired outcome for that response determined, then this would appear as the manager also having a proactive response to risk.

It would not be in the best interests of managers to address their responsibility using a reactive approach. This would suggest that processes are being carried out with no planning or scheduling of resources and without an objective. This approach would be ludicrous because there would be no planning, and managers would spend all of their time responding to process requirements. Unfortunately, this is, in fact, how many managers approach problems that come up, without identifying and planning for those problems beforehand.

Power Tool

Planning for problems is a proactive approach, whereas *responding to problems after they have occurred is a reactive approach* to risk management. How managers respond to problems is largely a statement of the culture the organization has in preparing for risk.

Culture of Risk Preparation

Just as it was the culture of those founding the organization to take risk, it was also part of that culture to plan for certain problems that might have occurred that would have had a high probability of happening and would have presented a great impact on the operation. With most organizations this culture stays with the founders and does not get trained within the rest of the management. This is unfortunate because *it was the planning of potentially serious problems that allowed the founders to move forward with developing the organization,* but the same planning is not a part of the day-to-day operation with midlevel managers, and therefore problems, great or small, continually plague the organization.

This type of training for risk management is not difficult or time-consuming, but simply requires managers to have some basic fundamental tools and knowledge of how planning for risk and problems can now be a part of the culture of the organization.

Power Tool

Planning for problems gives managers the confidence to oversee processes on a day-to-day level knowing that they have solutions planned for potential problems. This also *allows managers to embark on new responsibilities* they might acquire because they now have *a tool that enables them to plan for problems.*

This is how the culture of risk management is trained and implemented within an organization, improving the confidence and efficiency of those managing the organization. When risk management is carried out and the outcome of planning for problems is seen by others, this causes other management to follow this approach, and it becomes a part of the culture of the organization.

Cost of Doing Business

Although risk is a part of not only developing an organization but also managing the operation on a day-to-day basis, many of these risks can be identified and planned for. An equally important consideration is what happens when problems crop up that were not identified, or that were identified yet still happened and have to be dealt with. All that the best planning managers can do in risk management cannot completely prevent problems from happening. Risk management is more about identifying and planning for risk than it is about eliminating risk. As you will see in this chapter, there are several ways you can plan a response to a problem, most of which will impact the operation to some degree. This is included in the overall cost of doing business.

When managers develop a budget, they are estimating the cost of performing the processes within their department. In some cases, these costs might include extra overhead—rework and any added cost associated with ensuring that processes get completed. These budgets will also need to include monies allocated for the response to problems having an impact on the budget. If money is allocated ahead of time in case of certain potential risks, these funds will need to be spent only in the event the problem actually occurs. This type of planning should be desired by managers because it ensures that they will stay on budget, having additional funds allocated for potential serious problems that might occur.

Power Tool

Budgeting for risk gives managers confidence that they will *stay on budget* and will *have monies set aside for potential problems*.

This type of planning also is desired by most financial managers within the organization to better plan for operational expenses. Although operations and midlevel managers can submit budgets for financial planning, it is rare for these budgets to include contingency monies for potential serious risks that were planned for by the manager. This level of planning shows a higher level of maturity for an organization in more accurately estimating the cost of doing business.

Risk Versus Uncertainty

When we evaluate potential problems more closely, we discover that problems fall into one of two primary categories: problems that can be *identified* and problems that *cannot be identified.* Managers typically hear comments like "It just happened," "I never saw that coming," "It happened right out of the blue," or, "It was just a matter of time." Although these might be valid *perceptions* by those who have encountered the problem, it might be that the problems could have been identified and planned for, or these might have been situations that happened without warning.

When processes are carried out, there are many things that can happen that can slow down the process, cause it to break or stop functioning, or affect the output or deliverable in some way. If the resources performing these processes, other supporting staff, or subject matter experts were to walk through each component of the process, several potential problems could be identified.

In most cases managers and staff could generate an exhaustive list of potential problems with a wide range of probability of occurrence and impact on the process. There also could be myriad of other things that could happen in the physical universe that could have an impact but might not be as readily identifiable. These are broken down into two primary classifications: identifiable problems, called risk, and unidentifiable problems, called uncertainty.

Risk

Risk encompasses identifiable problems that can produce an unfavorable outcome. Potential problems can be found all throughout the organization and at all levels. These can be related to processes performed within a department, human resource issues, engineering or manufacturing issues, or the use of subcontractors, as well as management and decision-making issues. Risks can vary in size, having either a high or low probability of occurrence, as well as a great or small impact on the operation. Risks do not always result in a negative outcome; they can be an unexpected opportunity as well.

Because these problems can be identified, they can also be analyzed for their probability of occurrence and impact, and a response plan can be formulated. As part of the response plan, contingency efforts can result in finance and schedule planning as well. This can be a big help for the manager in estimating a budget, as well as in resource allocation. Developing a risk management plan is covered in the next section of this chapter.

Uncertainty

Uncertainty is simply an unexpected outcome. Uncertainties could be inconsistent variation, some component of a process that was not planned, or an "act of God" element. Uncertainty usually comes with an element of surprise—something happens that was completely unexpected. An example might be doing building construction in the middle of a desert, in the summer, and having a thunderstorm cause damage and delay. Although this could have been identified as a potential problem if this were conducted in the middle of winter, it would not be seen as a threat in the middle of summer and therefore would not have been identified as a problem. Although theoretically one could list every potential problem in the physical universe, therefore eliminating all uncertainty, this is not practical for the manager in risk management planning. Uncertainty can then be understood as problems with such a low probability of occurrence that it would be seen as a surprise if they occurred.

Risk Management Planning

In being prepared for potential problems, the manager must formulate a plan in how to approach problems that have a probability of occurrence and have a severity such that they would impact a schedule, budget, or deliverable. In developing the risk management plan, there are five fundamental areas the operations manager will want to consider:

1. Identify risks
2. Analyze risk
3. Plan response
4. Monitor and control
5. Audit and review

Note

Within project management, the risk management plan has five process steps: plan risk, identify, qualify, quantify, and plan risk response. Although these are more specific to project management, they are included in the previously listed areas of risk management for operations.

Identify and Document Risks

The first component in developing the risk management plan is identifying and documenting potential problems (risks). This is an important first step because this is where the manager gathers initial information about potential risks.

Power Tool

The *accuracy* and *completeness* of information is *critical* in developing an effective plan for potential risk.

It is advisable for managers to list individual areas of their department in which they would like to do risk management planning. It is best, in operations management, for the manager to have more individualized plans for specific processes within the department, rather than one large plan that covers everything. This will make it easier to manage response planning, monitoring, and contingencies. This will also help the manager identify only the risks for specific processes and keep the scope of the plan relative to that process.

Warning

The manager must be specific about what risks are being identified, for which process, and must ensure that the risk planning stays within the scope the manager has identified.

Risk identification is the process of accumulating information about potential problems that will have the manager answering five fundamental questions about risk—three that are covered in risk identification and two that are covered in risk analysis. These are the three fundamental areas within risk identification:

1. Who—Who will be performing the identification, and who will be interviewed to offer information?

2. What—What kinds of risks will there be, what are the sources of risk, and what is the potential impact and probability of occurrence?

3. When—When are risks expected to happen so that planning and scheduling of resources will be accurate?

Who

The manager first needs to identify the person or persons involved in developing the risk management plan. The manager might be the only one conducting this effort, or the manager could solicit the help of others in the department to help in gathering information, doing the analysis, and formulating the overall management plan. This is critical because those helping the manager need to understand the purpose in developing risk management so that the information that is gathered and analyzed will be useful in trying to mitigate or eliminate risk.

These individuals should be skilled or have experience in accurately gathering data from subject matter experts and doing simple analytical work to formulate the risk management plan. Because the risk management plan will work only as well as the accuracy of the data it is based on, it is imperative that these individuals understand how to gather data, what questions to ask, and the importance of detail within this information. The manager can also identify certain individuals whom she would like to train in performing risk information gathering and analysis, and these individuals can be assigned to do this occasionally throughout the department. These tools are covered later in this chapter in the section "Analyzing, Categorizing, and Prioritizing Risk."

The second part of *who* is involved is *what resources should be interviewed* for accurate information. If the manager is gathering information about a process, he must look to how the process was developed and the details around the process to best know who would understand problems relative to that process. Resources performing the process should be interviewed because they have firsthand knowledge and details of problems that could happen. Others who might have been involved in developing the process, such as manufacturing or process engineers or functional managers within the department, should be interviewed as well because they would know where potential problems would be or would know about problems that have happened in the past.

In the course of developing a process, problems do occur, and a process improvement was developed by someone to eliminate those problems; these same individuals would also know if these problems could still present potential risk. If subcontractors are used, they can be a wealth of information about potential problems that could happen, and they might be considered a subject matter expert. Contractors are typically hired based on the fact that they are perceived as professionals who have knowledge and experience of not only how to do something but the potential risks as well.

What

The second area the manager needs to consider is what type of potential problems there could be. This is where the manager needs to think out-of-the-box and, when information gathering, inspire imagination as to the variety of potential risks. This is accomplished during the information-gathering process with those who will be interviewed to get as much detail about potential risk as possible. Because these interviews can typically yield the very-high-probability and severe risks, they should be encouraged to think about the medium- and lower-level risks if possible.

In project management it's a typical understanding that just because risks are categorized as medium- or low-probability or severity doesn't mean that the classification can't change in the course of the project due to other influences. This is why all levels of risk should be identified so that they can be categorized and prioritized by probability and severity. They can also be planned for if the probability or severity is to change at a later date or under different circumstances.

When

The third area the manager will need to consider is at what point problems will likely occur. This is equally important because the manager needs to know not only what the problem is, but when the problem might happen because this can play a large role in the response plan. *When* a problem happens can also be a function of its impact on a process or within a department. For example, a software problem causing network downtime at one point in the day might impact only a couple of processes and therefore have minimal severity. If the network was to experience the same problem during critical applications, it might have a much higher impact and therefore be graded with a much higher severity. The same problem with the same probability of occurrence can have a drastically different impact on the operation depending on when it occurred.

The manager must then rely on tools to understand the impact that a potential risk might have relative to the timing within the operation or within a process. One tool might be process documentation that outlines the steps within a process that can reveal how severe a potential risk could be based on when it occurred. If the scope of risk identification is on a larger scale, a tool like the work breakdown structure might help identify over the course of several days, weeks, or months when potential risks would occur and the corresponding impact they would have. Tables 7.1 and 7.2 show two examples of how work breakdown structure could include potential risks on a special project or on a normal process giving the manager a way to plan risk.

Another tool a manager could use is called a Network Diagram. It also shows the sequence of process steps or tasks and where potential risks could occur to help in understanding the severity and impact of those risks. Figure 7.1 shows an example of how a Network Diagram can be used to not only identify but plan for risk events that might happen.

Table 7.1 Work Breakdown Structure for a Project with Risk Planning

Task	WBS Code	Project Tasks	Duration	Predecessor	Resources
1	1	**Project Name**	**33 Days Total**		
2	1.1	**First Subtask**	**14 Days Subtotal**		
3	1.1.1	Lower Divided Subtask or Work Package	2 Days		Name
		Possible Risk Event	**2-Day Delay**		
4	1.1.2	Lower Divided Subtask or Work Package	7 Days		Name
5	1.1.2.1		4 Days	3	Name
		Possible Risk Event	**1-Day Delay**		
6	1.1.2.2	Lowest Level Work Package	3 Days	5	Name
7	1.1.3	Lower Divided Subtask or Work Package	5 Days	6	Name
8	1.2	**Second Subtask**	**8 Days Subtotal**		
9	1.2.1	Lower Divided Subtask or Work Package	5 Days	7	Name
		Possible Risk Event	**1/2-Day Delay**		
10	1.2.2	Lower Divided Subtask or Work Package	3 Days	9	Name
11	1.3	**Third Subtask**	**11 Days Subtotal**		
12	1.3.1	Lower Divided Subtask or Work Package	7 Days	10	Name
		Possible Risk Event	**3-Day Delay**		
13	1.3.2	Lower Divided Subtask or Work Package	4 DAys	12	Name

Table 7.2 Work Breakdown Structure for a Process with Risk Planning

Task	WBS Code	Operations Processes	Duration	Duration w/Risk	Name
1	1	**Process Name**	**33 Days Total**		
2	1.1	**First Subtask**	**7 1/2 Hrs Total**	**8 3/4 Hrs Total**	
3	1.1.1	1st Sub-assembly	2 Hrs		
		Possible Risk Event	**45-Min Delay**		
4	1.1.2	2nd Sub-assembly	3 Hrs		
5	1.1.2.1	Secondary task	1 Hr		
		Possible Risk Event	**30-Min Delay**		
6	1.1.2.2	Secondary task	30 Min		
7	1.1.3	3rd Sub-assembly	1 Hr		
8	1.2	**Second Subtask**	**7 Hrs Total**	**9 Hrs Total**	
9	1.2.1	1st Sub-assembly	4 Hrs		
		Possible Risk Event	**2-Hr Delay**		
10	1.2.2	2nd Sub-assembly	3 Hrs		

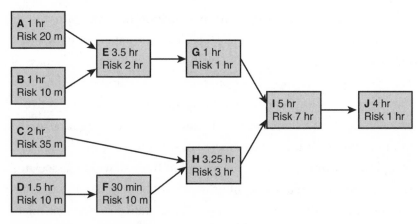

Figure 7.1 Network Diagram with risk planning.

Power Tool

The manager will have more confidence in day-to-day operations if *potential problems have been identified* and *response plans are in place.*

This does seem like extra work and in many cases is not necessary, but any manager who has experienced the power of having planned for a potential problem and having had that problem realized knows how good it feels to be prepared with a plan in place.

Analyze, Categorize, and Prioritize Risks

After risks have been identified, they must be analyzed to determine their probability of occurrence as well as impact on the process or department. The process of analyzing risks can be broken up into two primary approaches:

- **Qualitative**—More generalized, nonnumerical and subjective
- **Quantitative**—More specific, numerical and objective

In *qualitative risk assessment,* information that was gathered on specific risks might be in more a generalized format using less specific terms such as high, medium, or low; hot or cold; good or bad; pass or fail. Although these are descriptive enough for understanding risk, they do not have any numerical values and thus are more subjective in articulating the attributes of risk. In some cases, this might be all the information that is available to assess risk. Depending on the size and complexity of the process or environment the risk will be associated with, this level of analysis might or might not be suitable. In less complex environments, a more generalized qualitative assessment might be fine because it can provide a quick and basic assessment. In more complex environments or those that are more critical to the operation, a more in-depth, precise analysis with actual percentages and numbers is required.

Quantitative risk assessment is much more detailed, is objective, and usually results in percentages or other numerical values. If this level of information is available, it is always best to use a quantitative assessment because it will allow for better response planning and assessment of budgetary and schedule impact. If the manager will require actual cost data and numbers of days or weeks that will impact the schedule, this type of data needs to be obtained in the original information-gathering exercise.

Categorize

After an analysis has been performed on several risks within a process, the manager will need to categorize these risks to separate high and low probability as well as high and low impact. This, in most cases for operations managers, can be a relatively simple process, and developing a matrix enables the manager to take either qualitative or quantitative information and rank the risks in terms of probability and impact. A simple tool used in project management for doing this is called a *risk matrix.* As shown in Table 7.3, the risk matrix has more of a qualitative approach that allows for risks to be categorized and a very basic ranking associated with it to better understand which risks require more attention than others.

Table 7.3 Risk Matrix

Risk Assessment Matrix			
Risk	**Impact**	**Probability**	**Sum of Weight**
Shipments are delayed	High	Medium	5
Long lead time, hardware	Medium	Medium	4
Resource unavailable	Medium	Low	3
Rework problems	Low	Medium	3
	Low = 1	Medium = 2	High = 3

Prioritize

When risks have been categorized and a relative ranking has been assigned, it is time to prioritize the risks and document them in a form that will enable the manager to assign other pieces of information such as response planning, contingencies, and owners of these risks. This is an important step in taking all the information about the risks that have been identified, analyzed, and categorized and putting it into one place where the manager can easily monitor risks. This is also an important tool managers can use to effectively communicate the risk management plan to others in the department, as well as supporting staff such as manufacturing and process engineers, quality engineers, finance, HR, and other management staff.

This information is prioritized and documented in project management using a tool called a *risk register*. This register is again a simple tool managers can build that can identify several pieces of information about each risk in addition to the overall prioritization and response strategies. The risk register shown in Table 7.4 gives an example of some of the areas of information associated with each risk that the manager can assign or view.

Table 7.4 Risk Register

Risk Register

Risk Priority	Description	Probability	Impact	Risk Trigger	Response Strategy	Contingency Plan	Risk Owner	Event Entry Date	Response Due Date	Actual Response Date	Manager Notes
5	Shipments Delayed	M	H								
4	Hardware lead time	M	M								
3	Resource unavailable	L	M								
3	Rework problems	M	L								

The manager can customize her own risk register based on the complexity of process or risk monitoring she will need to have. In addition to the name of the risk and the associated probability and impact, other columns could include early indicators or triggers, the owner of the risk, expected timeframe, response plan, and/or contingency, as well as any other pertinent information the manager might want to include.

It's important for the manager to keep risks logged onto the risk register and to not remove any, because risks, even small, can still pose a threat with minimal probability or impact. As discussed earlier, risks can change in probability or impact relative to other influences that might alter the situation and recategorize a risk to a higher level.

Power Tool

The manager needs to *continue to monitor all the risks* to see whether any shift in priority in the risk register will be necessary. The *risk register is then the primary tool* the manager will use in monitoring potential risk.

Plan Response and Contingencies

After risks have been prioritized and placed in the risk register, response and contingency planning needs to be performed on each risk. Depending on the complexity of the environment and the severity and impact of the risks in the register, it might be decided that only high- and medium-priority risks will have actual contingency and response plans developed. If lower-prioritized risks have a relatively low impact on the project, it might be decided that these risks, although identified, can simply play out, having relatively little impact on cost or schedule but should still be monitored as a risk. With high- and medium-priority risks, a response plan is important because this will outline the steps that will take place should a problem be detected. Response plans are important, and there are four proactive ways to respond to any given risk:

- **Avoidance**—This plan identifies an alternative that will elimi-nate the risk completely. This is usually the best plan of action because it eliminates the effect the risk would have and any associated impact to the cost, schedule, or quality of a process. This might require thinking out-of-the-box as to a new way of doing something to eliminate a risk. It might also be simply a minor modification in an existing process that avoids a risk.

- **Mitigation**—This plan is only able to identify a reduction in probability or impact and not completely eliminate the risk. Mitigation plans for the risk to happen, which places all the importance on the response's being carried out accurately to minimize the impact of the risk.

- **Acceptance**—This plan is applied to risks that, after careful analysis and categorization, will likely have little impact based on severity. Acceptance assumes that the risk will play out with little or no response required, but will still be monitored for any shifts in severity. The cost, schedule, and quality impact in resource planning a response to avoid or mitigate this risk would cost more than simply letting the risk play out. This approach is left to the discretion of the manager as to the cost benefit in designing a response versus the overall cost the risk would have.

- **Transference**—This plan transfers the responsibility of risk and therefore the response or any contingency to a third party. This is commonly seen with the use of subcontractors who will assume the liability and risk of work being performed as defined by their contract. Any problems, setbacks, or added costs could be absorbed by the contractors based on the type of contract they have. Another form of transference is in the use of the organization's insurance policy, which could be engaged should a major risk event result in a severe impact to the organization.

Another element in response planning is that of early indicators or triggers that can be identified to help give early detection that a risk event or problem is imminent. These are typically found during information gathering from subject matter experts and those directly involved with the process. Early indicators or triggers can be information offered in status meetings or phone calls from suppliers or vendors that might produce critical first-sign information that a bigger problem might be on the horizon. In areas where equipment or machinery might be used, the first signs of fatigue, however small, might be all that is needed to understand a full-scale problem before it actually happens, causing catastrophic damage or injury.

When heavy equipment or machines have the first sign or trigger, in many cases, the manager has time to respond with a workaround or replacement machine or equipment until that one can be repaired, resulting in minimal cost and downtime. If these triggers were not recognized, problems could result in higher-cost solutions, downtime, and no time to plan a response to a major problem with a workaround. Early-detection triggers, no matter how small and insignificant, can ultimately be one of the most powerful pieces of information in the risk register.

Another column to include in the risk register in planning responses is selecting an owner of a risk item. It is important that each risk have an owner assigned who is knowledgeable about the details of the risk and who will be responsible for executing the response. It might not always be the manager; in many cases it might be the subject matter expert or resource directly involved with the process. Resources with firsthand, direct knowledge of the process and potential risks are generally the best first responders who can identify early-detection triggers or initiate a response plan quickly. If a resource is identified as the owner of a risk event, the manager needs to make sure that information has been communicated to the resource along with the response plan and any contingency plans that have been made. This also gives that resource ownership of that risk, as well as accountability in ensuring that the response and contingency are carried out correctly and completely.

Contingency Plan

Contingency planning is part of the response plan in the event that mitigation, acceptance, or transference has been selected. Contingencies are typically backup plans in case something happens that allow for the allocation of resources to carry out the response plan. If finances have been planned as part of a response, the accounting department needs to be aware of how much finances will be required and when they would be expected to be used if needed. If human resources or capital equipment will be required in a contingency plan, these also need to be scheduled so that they will be available to ensure that the response plan will be carried out effectively. Contingency plans are important in their development and in being communicated to the risk owner and associated departments within the organization.

Power Tool

The contingency plan gives the manager the response tool needed to *address risks confidently, in a timely manner, and cost-effectively.*

Monitor and Apply Controls

With potential risks identified, analyzed, categorized, and prioritized, and responses developed, the manager now has the risk management tools needed to effectively address risk within their department. This tool will be effective only if used on a daily basis or during critical processes requiring risk analysis in preparation. The only way the manager will know whether responses to risk are required is if the manager is monitoring departmental activities and processes. This will require the manager to put into place a monitoring system that would include detection, early warning triggers, and a communication method that can quickly and effectively transfer information of potential risks to the appropriate risk owners and/or managers for evaluation.

With monitoring systems in place and effective communication established, the manager also needs to ensure that the risk owners are aware of their responsibility with regard to established response plans and contingencies. In some cases, response plans might rely on avoidance or mitigation that involves critical early steps that need to be taken to effectively carry out that response.

Power Tool

These *early detections are control mechanisms* that are designed to *avoid problems* or to put into place early detection of problems so that avoidance or mitigation can be carried out.

These controls are vital and those responsible for the controls must be trained properly in their implementation and importance within the risk management plan.

Perform Audits and Reviews

Managers need to have some way of knowing that the risk management plan is effective and that the work involved in developing the risk management plan is justified. This will be available only through an audit and review system in which the effectiveness of response plans and contingencies are evaluated when used. Managers will also want to know whether they have correctly identified risk, have accurately analyzed risk, have developed effective response planning, and have controls in place to carry out risk monitoring and response plans. Managers should audit processes and areas within their department to see whether problems and risks have been avoided due to planning or have been mitigated, lessening the cost or schedule impact on the department.

Power Tool

When risk management planning is correctly developed and effectively implemented, managers will find that it *does reduce or eliminate potential problems, reduce cost, and maximize efficiency.*

Managers can also use this information to assess processes for improvement. One approach to process improvement is through reactive cost reduction, rework response, or efficiency improvement exercise. A better approach would be through the proactive assessment of potential problems that results in a response plan to avoid these problems, generating the necessity for process improvement. This not only accomplishes process improvement for cost reduction and efficiency, but also addresses potential risk. It will be this kind of forward-thinking, proactive-type approach to managing that takes the manager to the next level. It is always great to hear about a manager's response time and problem-solving skill, but it would be better to hear that due to the manager's planning, fewer responses are required! This gives the manager more time to focus on managing and planning, instead of running around fighting problems.

Learn from Your Experiences

One of the most powerful tools project managers use in making decisions is information from past projects. Some project managers use information from experience, while others with less experience or confidence will draw information from former projects or observing projects currently in progress. Managers have witnessed problems in the organization and this should be the warning call to pay attention. The information of past problems is there, the question is what to do with it.

Understand What Happened

There are two important components of developing and implementing a risk management plan:

- Understanding the importance of why the plan is developed
- Understanding the importance of the information generated from risk responses

All too often, organizations make mistakes, continue to have problems, and seem to reinvent the wheel over and over. This is unfortunate for organizations that have weathered problems, written off cost, and dealt with schedule delays only to have a culture that still *reacts to problems* versus *proactively avoiding problems.*

A competitive advantage many organizations do not consider is the power of the avoidance of problems or setbacks and the corresponding savings in finances, scheduling, and resources. When organizations review their business performance for overhead expenditures and productivity, it usually indicates the *effect that problems have had* on the operation. Risk response planning would then improve these numbers, resulting in a *savings* to the organization *in avoiding or minimizing risk.*

This is how the organization begins to develop a culture for risk management planning, through the understanding of the effect it will have in improving the organization's performance. This is also why executive management should drive this agenda as cost savings; schedule and resource management will be greatly improved, which will be seen in the overall bottom line! Executives get excited about these numbers and types of improvements within the organization.

Document What Happened

The risk management plan is not only about documenting the plan itself, but also about the outcome of any response plans or contingencies that were carried out. This is how the manager will not only report the success or failure of response plans and contingencies, but also fine-tune the risk management process, making it better. Like any other process, risk management planning has process development requirements as well. This is why the audit and review process is necessary to provide feedback to the manager on the effectiveness of the plan. In communicating response plans and contingencies that were successful, this allows for other management and senior management staff to become aware and more confident of the risk management plan approach.

Documenting risk events as they happen, and the effect that a response plan had, will serve as a lessons-learned document for others to review later. As mentioned, organizations should have a culture of learning from their mistakes and fine-tuning risk management plans to avoid future mistakes or problems. Documentation of actual risk events can also help in better estimating the cost and schedule impacts of similar risk events for future risk planning. This will be another source of information for identifying and analyzing risks as well as developing response plans to better understand the severity and impact risks can have within the operation.

Don't Let It Happen Again

The last important area in risk management planning is the effective communication of not only the risk response plans and contingencies, but also the effectiveness of the overall risk management plan approach. Proactively avoiding problems and future risk events can happen only when problems and risks have been experienced and response plans have been implemented that show how the organization can respond to problems effectively. When those engaged in the actual processes themselves see what potential problems can happen, it will help them understand their process better and help them identify other potential risks. This will in turn result in better identification of risks and information gathering of potential problems. This can also promote more awareness within the organization of what real impact problems can have on the organization's finances, schedules, and resources, as well as commitments to customers.

Power Tool

The manager developing and implementing the risk management plan will be *more in tune with processes and activities* conducted within the department, and can *confidently prepare* for any potential risks and significantly contribute to cost reduction *through problem mitigation and elimination.*

Power Tool Summary

- When managers are trained and educated and know how to identify and plan for problems, they can operate in a *proactive mode rather than a reactive mode.*

- *Planning for problems is a proactive approach,* whereas *responding to problems after they have occurred is a reactive approach* to risk management. How managers respond to problems is largely a statement of the culture the organization has in preparing for risk.

- *Planning for problems gives managers the confidence to oversee processes* on a day-to-day level knowing that they have solutions planned for potential problems. This also *allows managers to embark on new responsibilities* they might acquire because they now have a *tool that enables them to plan for problems.*

- Budgeting for risk gives managers confidence that they will *stay on budget* and will *have monies set aside for potential problems.*

- The *accuracy* and *completeness* of information is *critical* in developing an effective plan for potential risk.

- The manager will have more confidence in day-to-day operations if *potential problems have been identified* and *response plans are in place.*
- The manager needs to *continue to monitor all the risks* to see whether any shift in priority in the risk register will be necessary. The *risk register is then the primary tool* the manager will use in monitoring potential risk.
- The contingency plan gives the manager the response tool needed to *address risks confidently, in a timely manner, and cost-effectively.*
- These *early detections are control mechanisms* that are designed to *avoid problems* or to put into place early detection of problems so that avoidance or mitigation can be carried out.
- When risk management planning is correctly developed and effectively implemented, managers will find that it *does reduce or eliminate potential problems, reduce cost, and maximize efficiency.*
- The manager developing and implementing the risk management plan will be *more in tune with processes and activities* conducted within the department, and can *confidently prepare* for any potential risks and significantly contribute to cost reduction *through problem mitigation and elimination.*

8

Synergy in Management

As organizations are founded, structured, and organized, one thing will not change any time soon: Organizations will have managers to oversee the operation. These resources overseeing the operations can be at various levels, from the owners or officers to mid- and lower-level management. One source of stress and potential problem within an organization can be the relationships between managers and/or upper management. If an organization was divided into departments that could all work independently of each other, this would not be as big a problem, but departments within organizations will have managers who have to work together or be connected in some way and relationships will be formed. As managers, you know that there are other managers in the organization you get along with very well, whereas there are other managers with whom you have more of a *challenging* working relationship. Relationships would not be as big a problem if you did not conduct much business with that person. If you have to conduct business with a person on a regular basis and the relationship is strained, the business might not be as efficient or as effective as it could be.

Managerial Behavior

The behavior of managers can stem from some several different influences. Managerial behavior is a response from pressure that forces managers to react in a favorable manner or not. Behaviors might be an inherent characteristic of their personality or a result of situations outside the workplace. Behaviors might also be a result of agendas that managers are trying to push, or the compulsion to move up in management and therefore respond differently than other managers who do not aspire to move up the corporate ladder with such vigor. Whatever the reason, managers are going to have and will display behaviors when working with each other, and how these behaviors are manifested and managed can play a big role in the overall success of a manager and the organization.

As a leadership figure in the organization, managers have to understand that they are a visible icon of some level of management and will be viewed, primarily by those working around them, as an example of not only management but leadership. The example of the typical level-headed manager is the goal, but this is easier said than done because there are many things that can influence a manager in the course of a day. There are responsibility-related influences and relationship-related influences. Managers will be constantly evaluating these as they manage in three directions:

1. **Manage you—your own time and activities**—As both an employee and a manager, you find that there will be certain responsibilities that need to be scheduled and managed to best utilize your time during the work day. This can pose a stress because both organizational and outside commitments and relationships can require time and force the manager to choose, which can cause unwanted behaviors. This also goes into the area of managing stress because this can be an influence that can play a large role in how behaviors play out.

2. **Manage below—things you have responsibility for**— For managers there are responsibilities as a function of the job, such as managing processes as well as human resources, departmental schedules, and commitments, that can generate stress. Managers have to respond to problems in the work flow of processes, but it seems that dealing with human resource

problems or relationships can be more difficult and can cause certain behaviors.

3. **Manage above—management above you**—Managers typically do not think they are managing staff above them in the course of their work, but this is the case and is okay! Members of upper management want to be updated on the status of work flow and personnel issues but generally want only the higher-level information and not the details. Knowing what they want is a way of managing them as you are proactive in how you approach, discuss, and report the status of the department. Not understanding upper management is typically a source of stress for managers and can be a cause of certain behaviors, especially in management meetings.

Managerial Diversity

In most organizations, members of senior and executive management foster, promote, and enjoy the diversity among midlevel management because this brings character to the company and in many ways helps make the company stronger. There is also a responsibility to ensure that although managers have varying personalities and temperaments, they can still be professional and work together for the overall benefit of the organization.

Part of team skills training is the strength in the diversity of a team. There needs to be a mutual respect for various backgrounds, experience, views, and opinions that fosters open-minded thinking and variety in thought processes.

Power Tool

In *allowing for diversity,* managers cultivate an environment that *encourages out-of-the-box thinking* and really looking at *all* the options to come to the best conclusion for a decision.

This is one way organizations do well in developing great game plans, and they seem to have cutting-edge type approaches as they allow the personalities to work freely together and not fight.

Although this can make sense in theory, it is difficult in practice because all the managers have to participate in this type of thinking and understanding in their relationships with each other. This is when organizations start to mature, progress happens, and power in completion is realized, because things are not only getting done, but getting done really well!

Managerial Relationships

Synergy within management can be at various levels and can take on different degrees of relationship between midlevel management, executive-level management, and upper management, as well as among peer managers at the same level. Management has to meet, discuss, and decide how the organization will be run and to report on the status of objectives, budgets, and schedules, as well as special tasks or projects that are being completed. So how does synergy in the relationships of these managers affect a manager's power or control within an organization and ability to be successful?

This, for the most part, starts as a top-down philosophy in which the senior and executive management discuss the strategic business plan of the organization and come to an agreement about how it will be implemented. They then need to effectively communicate that plan to midlevel management so that managers can see that upper management is in agreement about a direction the businesses is going and have a clear understanding of their objective within their particular department. When executive management agrees on an objective, there is synergy between those managers that can be seen and felt by the rest of the organization, which gives credibility not only to the decision they made but the managing group itself in their ability to run the organization.

Executive management can then communicate an objective to midlevel management to carry out in the department, and it will be believable and more accepted by midlevel managers.

Power Tool

It is vitally important that midlevel management *see the synergy of executive management* producing a cohesive decision. This *encourages a synergy among the midlevel management* that is seen by the working staff, giving credibility to the decisions being made by management and within the department.

It's not so much the decision that was made, but the fact that there was synergy among the management in that decision that drives the rest of the organization to believe in an objective.

This synergy comes at a price, because in management meetings and in discussing an objective, there is *not* always agreement at the onset. This is when the organization's management show their true colors and maturity in being able to conduct meetings and come to an agreement that allows the organization to move forward. This is what helps not only the managers but also the organization actually complete tasks and see objectives through to completion, giving the organization true power through this completion process.

Power Tool

This power can be realized as management *becomes more mature* and *understands what effect they have on the rest of the organization,* not only in their behavior and attitude, but also in how they appear to the rest of the organization in being able to manage decisions.

Within most organizations it's common that many people will know how management feels about any given objective or direction based on the behaviors and attitudes of the managers. If managers at either the midlevel or the executive level are not in agreement about the direction of the department or organization, this can be seen by others who work with those management staff. This can create an atmosphere of distrust in management, with others questioning their ability or process as a team to come to an agreeable conclusion. This is where managers might disagree, due to personality conflicts or strong feelings, about whether a direction is the best course of action.

There might be cases in which a manager is lobbying for his own agenda that would result in some form of reward, gain, or notoriety for him. This should be unacceptable behavior by managers because this potentially divides the management staff and does not allow the organization to run smoothly and effectively. This can even create tension and trouble between managers, resulting in arguments that are not constructive that would normally bring out the positive and negative sides of everyone's view. In most cases managerial meetings are best and most effective when all managers participating are able to share their views and all ideas, and when brainstorming efforts can be put out on the table for discussion.

The mature management team has the ability to move through a selection and elimination process that allows them to collectively narrow down ideas to a single element that everyone can agree on. One problem that management staff can have arises when certain managers are unable to let go of their idea, unable to compromise, unable to see the benefit of others' ideas, and they choose to hold onto their own idea as the only way. They are thus dividing the group and not allowing for synergy. This is when management teams become weak and begin to break down the organization's strengths in being able to effectively manage. So what tools are available to help promote synergy within a peer management group and between management levels?

Communication System

The first tool is in the communication structure formatting of how information is moved throughout the organization. In evaluating communication within an organization, project, or task, we need to break this down into subcomponent areas:

- What
- Who
- How
- When

What

This area involves the actual information that will be distributed. It is important to know what communication truly needs to be distributed and what communication simply needs to be documented and filed. Information is one of the building blocks of an organization because it can include the organizational structure, financial and legal information, employee documentation, customer and sales information, product and engineering data, drawings and test results, procurements, manufacturing and inventory information, and many other critical areas of an organization.

All of this information exists within the organization for a reason, but people need only the information required for their level of responsibility. Everyone in the organization will need information of some kind, and managers are responsible for determining what information various people will get and why. It is also important for information to be accurate, legible, and in a form that can be easily understood by the recipient. *Information has to be clear to be used correctly!*

Who

Not everyone in the organization needs to know all the information about everything in every department. It can be detrimental within an organization if the wrong people are getting the wrong information for the wrong reasons. This can cause midlevel managers and/or upper-level managers to make decisions based on incorrect information, too much information and detail, or possibly not enough information, resulting in mistakes based on poor communication. There might be cases in which other midlevel managers might not need to know certain pieces of information and therefore be compelled to be a part of a conversation, be included in threaded discussions, or join in on meetings they really do not need to attend. Too much detail might be communicated to executive management; or they might not understand what's actually happening or might misunderstand what was being communicated. Upper-level managers who have requested more detail or are simply not getting enough detail will still be required to make decisions, but those will be based on incorrect data.

Power Tool

It is important for an effective evaluation to be made as to *who is getting what type of information.*

How

This is the actual media via which the information will be sent based on the needs or requirements of the recipient. People might prefer an e-mail correspondence or might ask to sit in on a conference call rather than attending a meeting. In other cases people want the human interaction and ability for discussion and explanation you would get in a face-to-face meeting, and they feel this is a better form of communication than simply receiving an e-mail.

Power Tool

Knowing the recipient's preferred form of information delivery can be vital in improving and optimizing communication of information.

With regard to synergy within management, in many cases managers receive enough information via e-mail to be able to review and satisfy their need for understanding the status of that particular situation, whereas had they attended a meeting, they would have received too much information and been involved in discussions and possibly arguments based solely on the type of communication they received.

When

This area encompasses the logistics of time management because managers and executive management have limited time they can spend in meetings. Time management is a key area in controlling your time as a manager, and consideration must be given to how many meetings the manager attends, for what reasons, and what the manager plans to gain by attending certain meetings. This is partially the responsibility of the meeting planner, who should make sure that she invites only the people who "need" to be there. This is also the responsibility of the attending manager, to determine whether their attendance is needed as well. How often meetings are planned is important to both effective communication and time management.

Power Tool

Meeting attendance is a balance that project managers have to deal with and managers have to contend with as well. As we have seen, there are *critical updates and information that need to be communicated,* but *to the right people and at an effective frequency rate.*

Having too many meetings does not allow for enough information to be accumulated to justify a meeting, whereas having too infrequent meetings allows too much time to pass between updates. The amount of time elapsed between meetings is important because if too much time goes by, critical information is not communicated quickly and decisions that have to be made might run the risk of being too late.

Communication is important at all levels of management in the organization. Understanding the four primary communication elements within an organization—what information has to be communicated, to whom, how it will be communicated, and how often—is vital. Addressing the relationships that managers have among themselves and at various levels will help to improve the overall synergy within management. Because project managers have a complex communication responsibility, they must effectively manage the four elements of communication, organized in a tool called a Communications Matrix, shown in Table 8.1.

Power Tool

Having tools like the Communications Matrix helps *organize the what, who, how, and when elements* we have looked at.

Table 8.1 Communication Matrix

Communication Matrix				
Resource Type	Meetings to Attend	Frequency	Preferred Delivery	Correspondence
VP of Division	Management Status	Weekly	Face to Face/E-mail	Meeting Minutes
Facilities Manager	Management Status	Weekly	Face to Face/E-mail	Meeting Minutes
	Safety Committee	Monthly	Face to Face/E-mail	Meeting Minutes/ Action List

Communication Matrix				
Resource Type	Meetings to Attend	Frequency	Preferred Delivery	Correspondence
Engineering Manager	Management Status	Weekly	Conf Call/E-mail	Meeting Minutes
	Documentation Review	Monthly	Face to Face/E-mail	Meeting Minutes/ Docs for Review
	Safety Committee	Monthly	Conf Call/E-mail	Meeting Minutes/ Action List
	Project Status Review	As Needed	Conf Call/E-mail	Meeting Minutes/ Action List
Project Manager	Project Status Review	As Needed	Face to Face/E-mail	Meeting Minutes/ Action List
HR & Accounting Manager	Management Status	Weekly	Face to Face/E-mail	Meeting Minutes
Dept Supervisors	Dept General Communications	Bimonthly	Face to Face	Announcements/ Topic Discussions
	Dept Supervisor Update	Weekly	Face to Face/E-mail	Meeting Minutes/ Action List

This tool categorizes the what, who, how, and when for good communications and allows the manager to better organize communication within his department.

Needs of the Manager

Managers need to know many things—what they are responsible for, who is performing the processes in their department, and the flow of information are just a few of the things managers need to know to be successful. Managers at both the midlevel and the executive level need to understand how effective their department is at carrying out tasks and how efficiently their department is actually running. Managers have a requirement and need for information, a need for status, and the need to know that the human resources that have been chosen are correct and have the right skills for the tasks they have been assigned.

Managers need to know that correct information is being communicated and channels have been established that will optimize the quality and efficiency of communication. Managers also need to know what will be expected of them in the short term so that they can begin to plan within their department as to how they will organize their resources for upcoming objectives. Executive managers need to ensure that the strategic objectives of the organization are being carried out and that they have the right resources in place to meet those goals. Midlevel managers need to understand what they can do to help executive management in meeting those strategic objectives within their department.

Being Successful

The general understanding is that most midlevel and executive-level members of management want to, or have the need to, be successful. The tool for the manager is the basic understanding that in order to be successful there has to be a need inside of the manager to want to be successful, which drives the need to obtain tools to help the manager become successful. This attitude of being successful really starts from within. If you question whether a management position is right for you, either you do not really want the position or you want it but simply lack confidence. If you really don't think you are right for the position and question your managerial ability, this is normal if you have not previously had a management position and feel as though you are going through uncharted territory. You might want to seek the advice of other managers or do some research in managing to help determine whether that responsibility is for you.

If you really want a management position and are just not sure, this usually stems from a lack of knowledge and confidence. This is normal, and with training, time, and experience you will get better.

Power Tool

It's also vital for managers to understand a primary concept within managing: To help in being a successful manager, you should *surround yourself with successful people, understand the managerial responsibility, and develop leadership attributes.*

If you look at other midlevel managers or peer management as being working professionals who are all there for the common goal of making the organization successful, this can begin to form a synergy among management. If you understand that the members of executive management overseeing midlevel management are successful people and are in place for the common goal of making a successful organization, this will foster a synergy among the levels of management staff. This synergy really is the driving force behind how managers behave—how they respond and react to each other. How things as simple as meetings are carried out and conducted will speak to the general professionalism and maturity of the management staff.

It is the desire to be successful that starts within a new manager that drives success in what you do.

Power Tool

If you are not convinced that you are a success, it will be difficult for you to be successful. Developing tools, developing managerial skills, and looking at the organization through successful eyes is how successful managers *become successful and are sustainable as successful managers.*

Power Tool Summary

- In *allowing for diversity,* managers cultivate an environment that *encourages out-of-the-box thinking* and really looking at *all* the options to come to the best conclusion for a decision.

- It is vitally important that midlevel management *see the synergy of executive management* producing a cohesive decision. This *encourages a synergy among the midlevel management* that is seen by the working staff, giving credibility to the decisions being made by management and within the department.

- This power can be realized as management *becomes more mature* and *understands what effect they have on the rest of the organization,* not only in their behavior and attitude, but also in how they appear to the rest of the organization in being able to manage decisions.

- It is important for an effective evaluation to be made as to *who is getting what type of information.*

- *Knowing the recipient's preferred form of information delivery* can be vital in improving and optimizing communication of information.

- Meeting attendance is a balance that project managers have to deal with and managers have to contend with as well. As we have seen, there are *critical updates and information that need to be communicated,* but *to the right people and at an effective frequency rate.*

- Having tools like the Communications Matrix helps *organize the what, who, how, and when elements* we have looked at.

- It's also vital for managers to understand a primary concept within managing: To help in being a successful manager, you should *surround yourself with successful people, understand the managerial responsibility, and develop leadership attributes.*

- *If you are not convinced that you are a success, it will be difficult for you to be successful.* Developing tools, developing managerial skills, and looking at the organization through successful eyes is how successful managers *become successful and are sustainable as successful managers.*

9

Tamper-Proof Training

Organizations are more likely to be successful when human resources performing processes, as they were designed, are efficient at completing the processes. To ensure that human resources are at their most efficient, they need to have the right tools to do their job and be placed in a job they are educated for or have experience in, allowing them to perform at their peak. One area that is easily overlooked and underdeveloped is instructing the resource on the details of how to perform a process or training. You have been studying tools that can be used at the managerial level, and one of the most important tools, and fundamental to success, is training. Managers at all levels need to be trained in areas they are responsible for to be as effective as possible. Because managers will perform several duties within their job description, they too will need to follow processes and procedures that have been established for that department within the organization.

Training Is a Process

Managers need to understand that following processes ensures that they are doing a task correctly, the way it was designed. This promotes organization, completion, and efficiency, as well as standardization within the department. For the manager overseeing work carried out within a department, it should be of utmost importance to ensure that everyone working within the department is following the correct processes and procedures. Managers need to lead by example in doing the same. Managers should realize what a powerful tool proper training is and how much power they have in efficiency, completion, and control of their department when processes are followed.

Training is a process that also has to be developed and monitored to ensure that it is performed correctly. When training is viewed as a process, it can include development of the task steps, testing for verification, documentation, and monitoring the process to ensure that it is yielding the desired outcome. This starts by understanding what the process of training is trying to accomplish. Training is simply effectively communicating process tasks, through verbal explanation; written documentation; illustrations; and computer, Web-based, or hands-on exposure. The trainee needs to understand the process steps, in detail and sequence, as well as the reason the process exists and the importance it has in the organization.

Power Tool

The process of training, like any other process, *is best performed* and repeated *when there is a documented plan.*

Training Plan

When you're considering the process of training, it's best to try to keep it as simple as possible to avoid confusion and unnecessary steps. As with other processes, it's best to have someone skilled in process development to help outline the steps needed to effectively deliver training. This will also require a subject matter expert and in this case someone skilled in training. This is vitally important because people learn differently and there are several ways training can be administered. The development of a training approach is called the *training plan.* The basic areas of training need to be defined to implement the process effectively. When managers decide to evaluate the effectiveness of training within their department, they look to these five areas of the process:

1. **Implementation**—Develop a plan of the steps taken during the training process.

2. **Documentation**—Acquire and train from documentation that defines the process that will be trained.

3. **Qualified trainers**—Have someone qualified in training deliver the training.

4. **Delivery system**—Develop a delivery approach that matches the needs of the trainees.

5. **Monitoring and assessment**—Monitor actual performance and assess the progress of the trainee.

Implementation

The first area involves how training is actually implemented. Training is implemented in two primary forms:

1. Documented process communication

2. Undocumented process communication

In a *documented process*, training is implemented based on a well-designed process that has been thoroughly documented. Staff attends training sessions where this documentation is presented and gone through in detail, and staff is effectively trained on a process.

In an *undocumented process*, training is through the passing down of undocumented information or tribal knowledge—people in the department simply are told how to do something by somebody else. That person later trains somebody else verbally off the top of their head, and so on. There are some companies that have passed down information for decades never having once written down a process or procedure but simply passing on the information year after year as people are hired.

There are several inherent risks with undocumented process training:

- Information was not correct at the beginning, but was passed down anyway. *"The way we've always done it."*

- The trainer does not articulate the details about the process very well and leaves out steps, only to have the new person fill in those steps on their own through trial and error.

- If more than one person is training, there will be inconsistency in how the process is explained.

- Trainers can input their own opinion of how a process should be performed, efficient or not.

- The only person who knows the process left the organization, so now what?

Unfortunately, this is still the process in some organizations today, and in most cases, as a result of poor training practices, employees do not have all the information or tools they need to effectively do their job.

This is unfortunate because new employees usually want to be trained properly, want to have the right tools, and truly want to do the best they can in their performance. For the manager, having these training practices in the department unfortunately results in poorly trained employees who are not performing as effectively as they could, and this poses a problem for the manager in completing departmental processes, goals, and objectives.

Documentation

Documentation of processes and procedures is vital within an organization because this clearly states and records how procedures are actually done, by design, and allows for more accurate and consistent training of new resources. Documentation at many companies falls by the wayside and is not a high priority for managers because it requires resources skilled in technical writing that can clearly articulate in written form how procedures should be done. That is not to say that departmental managers have to wait to document something until they have a resource capable of doing the documentation. It would be nice to have that skill set in the department because most managers do not have this level of skill available and have to assign the task to other resources to try to document process as best they can.

Power Tool

The documentation of a process can be *as simple as taking pictures of a process* and *cutting and pasting those* into something like a Word document for people to visually see. Always train from documentation.

Illustrations such as a screenshot on a computer or a digital photograph of a physical item on a bench would help the trainee visualize that step in the process. This can be a way in which resources unskilled in writing might be able to build training documents that would be very effective. The point of this chapter is to point out *the importance of training and proper documentation* within the organization to *eliminate the risk of employees doing processes incorrectly* and not allowing for the department to be efficient and effective in accomplishing its objectives.

Qualified Trainers

As you have seen, there are five important areas to develop the training plan, and addressing the trainer is one of the most important. This is also another area organizations do not put enough emphasis on, and for good reason. Organizations, in streamlining the operation, do not have extra resources waiting around to train people, and not everyone can train! Trainers are resources who will facilitate communicating how a process will be performed to someone who has never done that process but has been assigned the task. In many organizations it's a common practice to take staff experienced with the process and utilize them as a trainer with the expectation that in knowing the process well they would be the ones best suited to train the process. This unfortunately is not always the case; the person might be an expert in the process but not very good at effectively communicating all the steps in the process.

Power Tool

The trainer should ensure that *all* the process steps have been effectively communicated to the trainee, such that they have *the most accurate information* and have received that information *in a manner they understand and remember.*

The trainer is a vital step in the training process because he is the key tool of communication. The trainer needs to have certain skills that go beyond the subject matter expert that will help the training process be successful. They must be able to do the following:

1. Understand the value of the *training plan approach.*

2. Insist on *training from documentation,* so documenting a process might have to happen.

3. Have the ability to *effectively communicate* details of process steps, not just talk about them.

4. Understand that *people learn in different ways,* at various speeds, and have varying levels of understanding and memory retention.

5. Be able to *monitor the trainee* during training for attention, questions, stress, and general understanding of the process.

6. *Have listening skills* to determine by verbal or body language that the recipient is receiving the communication clearly.

7. Be able to *adjust the training delivery method* on the fly if it is not effective.

8. Have a *feedback system* to assess the level of understanding by observing the trainee performing the task.

The trainer has to be knowledgeable not only about the subject, but also about how to interact and communicate effectively with people. So, as you have seen, there is more involved in properly training than just telling someone the steps of a process.

Power Tool

Effective training goes much deeper than just relaying the process steps. Having an *organized plan, a solid delivery method, and good communication techniques, as well as observing the trainee,* all play an *important role in a trainer's success.*

Delivery System

The next area is how the training will be delivered and the approach taken. The delivery and approach of training is much the same as the process of selecting the correct trainer based on their knowledge of the process and their communication skills. People understand information in different ways. Some people can be told something and understand it well, whereas for others, reading something, seeing a picture of something, or the hands-on approach is best. This is an important point to understand because the delivery and approach of training can vary depending on the staff who will be trained, their skill level, their educational level, and their general ability to receive and understand information.

Power Tool

The delivery system should *match the needs of the recipients* and what will *most likely be effective for the bulk of the recipients.* This will require some assessment and in some cases trial and error on the trainer's part.

Power Tool

A good trainer will *be perceptive as to how the trainees are receiving information* and whether they are comprehending and remembering what is being taught.

A process or procedure should always be documented, and then a delivery system can be evaluated to best communicate the information effectively. Trainers must be knowledgeable about the connection between the subject matter and the delivery method to derive a general feeling of how information will be accepted by the trainees. This can be visibly seen in a training session in the attentiveness of the trainees. Asking questions about what was just covered and elements covered earlier in the training will assess the trainees' understanding and retention of material. Having the trainee restate a sequence of components of the process can assess how much detail she is actually grasping. This will give the trainer an understanding as to the effectiveness of that particular type of delivery system.

If the trainer chooses a delivery system in which they sit and read through a document with the trainee, the trainer needs to have a feedback system to assess the trainee's interpretation of what they read to gauge the learner's understanding of the process. The trainer might want to look for signs of boredom or the trainee falling asleep or looking disinterested and fidgeting around because this would indicate that the trainee does not do well in reading documentation. The trainer might need to switch the delivery method to a slide presentation or graphics that would pictorially illustrate forms of the process to see whether this would improve the understanding and retention. If the trainer is still seeing signs that the trainee does not like this form of communication, the trainer might take the person to where the task is being performed and go through the process using a hands-on format.

Developing supporting documents to a process procedure can help the trainer communicate detailed information about process steps.

Power Tool

One example of a supporting document might simply be a series of pages that have *digital pictures showing the process* step-by-step with very little or no text associated with it.

Having pictorial process documentation allows the trainee to see the actual process material or visualize the processes being conducted and to get the sensation of touch and of performing the task before being allowed to actually perform the process. This allows them to understand more detail of the process and usually results in much higher retention of the process information. This can be a very effective tool because people have a tendency to remember pictures, colors, shapes, and sizes.

Power Tool

Trainees with the ability to *watch the process and/or perform the process with the supervision of a trainer* also have improved retention of process steps.

When a trainer is using a hands-on method, it's best to have the trainer perform the process first while the trainee observes the steps done correctly. Then the trainee can perform the same process steps with the trainer observing to ensure that the trainee has captured the details of the process. This form of hands-on training works well in a one-on-one situation or in training groups of no more than two or three at a time.

The effectiveness of this training lies solely on the trainee's being able to perform the process under the close supervision of the trainer and the focused attention the trainer can give. This approach might not be as effective in a large group scenario because it will be difficult for the trainer to give one-on-one attention to each trainee. When training is required for a large number of people, the classroom setting might be a better starting point to go through a process and have a blend of documentation with text explanations and pictures showing the process.

Power Tool

Another effective *large-group approach might use a video display, PowerPoint presentation, or flip charts* so that the trainer can talk to the class in more of a classroom setting.

The classroom approach can work in conjunction with small break-out sessions of two or three at a time to go through a process using the hands-on method because the class has already been exposed to the process steps but just need the practice. It is the responsibility of the manager to ensure that trainers who have been chosen for training within a department understand the basic concepts of training so that they can be most effective in the training approach, delivery, and assessment.

There might be instances in which trainers are sent to a location to train and they do not speak the language, or they might be in a different culture, which can present another level of complexity within the training plan.

Power Tool

The most effective tool in this approach is to have *written documentation in both languages* in which each paragraph or each sentence in the document is in the trainer's language followed by the same text in the trainee's language. This allows the trainer and the trainee to read through a document at the same time, understanding it in their own language. The use of pictures can also play a big role in conveying process step details and information that doesn't need to be interpreted.

The use of photographs of the process environment, digital pictures of the materials and tools, or screenshots of a computer are much more effective when training cross-culture or -languages. Pictures require very little text for explanation if they are done correctly and can illustrate and present each step of a process slowly and in detail. These are very important tools that will assist the manager in selection of appropriate trainers, correct documentation of processes, and delivery method and approach. The manager has the responsibility of ensuring that processes are being performed correctly and employees have the right tools and training they need in order to be efficient and successful.

Monitoring and Assessment

Measuring and assessing is an important area within the training process because the trainer can't really be sure that the trainee has completely grasped the details of the process and will have long-term retention, not requiring further training. Trainees can be very good at replicating process steps using short-term memory, having simply to respond to the trainer directly after being shown how to do something. Unfortunately, this does not indicate how long the trainee will remember the details of the process or whether they can remember all the process steps at all over a period of time. This is important for trainers to understand because many times the trainer performs the training function and moves on to other tasks assuming that the person understands it "well enough." It should not be assumed that people are ready to perform a process just because they completed the training; there must be a verification system that tests the knowledge of the trainee. Trainers can best accomplish this by setting up a monitoring plan to view the performance of trainees and assess their capabilities.

Power Tool

In the best-case scenario, someone who has been trained on a process *who starts the process immediately and performs only that process, not being assigned any other task, has a much higher probability of remembering* the process steps.

If that is all that the trainee has been tasked to do and they therefore can focus on just the tasks they've been trained on, this helps the trainee focus on retention of the process details. In many cases resources will be doing more than one process and will need to be trained on several processes. This makes it vitally important to avoid too much information that would be overwhelming for the trainee and cause confusion. Managers must realize that new employees or employees being transferred to another department will require time in the training process.

Power Tool

If *quality is to be built into the training process*, trainees need to *move more slowly through a process* at first *and perform it several times* to ensure that they understand and remember the process steps.

The trainer should stay in touch with the trainee after the training process to monitor how well he is doing. The trainer can then assess whether the trainee needs any follow-up training to help him better understand or remind him about process steps he might have forgotten or possibly misunderstood.

Monitoring and measuring can be used not only for assessing the performance of a trainee, but also to gauge how well the training materials have been developed for effectiveness in training that process. This will also give an indication as to the effectiveness of the trainer and whether the right person has been selected for the training process. It is important for the trainee to understand that the organization takes training seriously, and ongoing monitoring of training helps ensure that the employee is doing the process correctly and is getting the best training.

Managers need to understand their responsibility in managing the process of training, selection of trainers, and training material as being important in the success of the organization. Although this fosters good training practices, not everyone is cut out to be a trainer, and managers need to understand which resources are better suited for this type of job.

Power Tool

It's important that you, as a manager, *develop trainers within the department* who are *effective and successful at training.*

Having good trainers allows the flexibility of having new people brought into the department because there's a higher level of confidence that new people will be trained efficiently and correctly. This also allows the manager better control of process staffing and scheduling, giving the manager more control of the department and power in completing processes.

Power Tool Summary

- The process of training, like any other process, *is best performed* and repeated *when there is a documented plan.*

- The documentation of a process can be *as simple as taking pictures of a process* and *cutting and pasting those* into something like a Word document for people to visually see. Always train from documentation.

- The trainer should ensure that *all* the process steps have been effectively communicated to the trainee, such that they have *the most accurate information* and have received that information *in a manner they understand and remember.*

- Effective training goes much deeper than just relaying the process steps. Having an *organized plan, a solid delivery method, and good communication techniques, as well as observing the trainee,* all play an *important role in a trainer's success.*

- The delivery system should *match the needs of the recipients* and what will *most likely be effective for the bulk of the recipients.* This will require some assessment and in some cases trial and error on the trainer's part.

- A good trainer will *be perceptive as to how the trainees are receiving information* and whether they are comprehending and remembering what is being taught.

- One example of a supporting document might simply be a series of pages that have *digital pictures showing the process* step-by-step with very little or no text associated with it.

- Trainees with the ability to *watch the process and/or perform the process with the supervision of a trainer* also have improved retention of process steps.

- Another effective *large-group approach might use a video display, PowerPoint presentation, or flip charts* so that the trainer can talk to the class in more of a classroom setting.

- The most effective tool in this approach is to have *written documentation in both languages* in which each paragraph or each sentence in the document is in the trainer's language followed by the same text in the trainee's language. This allows the trainer and the trainee to read through a document at the same time, understanding it in their own language. The use of pictures can also play a big role in conveying process step details and information that doesn't need to be interpreted.

- In the best-case scenario, someone who has been trained on a process *who starts the process immediately and performs only that process, not being assigned any other task, has a much higher probability of remembering* the process steps.

- If *quality is to be built into the training process,* trainees need to *move more slowly through a process* at first *and perform it several times* to ensure that they understand and remember the process steps.

- It's important that you, as a manager, *develop trainers within the department who are effective and successful at training.*

10

The Weakest Link

When we think of a weak link, we generally picture a chain with one link that has been compromised and is about to break. The chain might be very strong and capable of great things, but one link stands in the way of that being able to happen. We can use the same analogy with an organization and what it's capable of doing, given the resources, but is not able accomplish because of weak links. Weak links would suggest that there is something substandard or not quite right with either human resources or processes within the organization.

This chapter is intended not to point fingers or place blame on individuals but rather to shed light on where possible improvements can be made and where certain critical areas in the organization might be weak, causing areas to suffer. Organizations are built or structured around processes, and as you have seen, the success of the organization is largely dependent on the development and implementation of these processes. As you have also seen, processes are simply a group of work tasks that accomplish a desired objective when complete. If one task in the sequence of tasks is not being performed correctly, it can appear as a weak link and adversely affect the whole process.

When looking at weak links within the organization, it must first be determined that you are simply looking for an area of work that has a higher probability to negatively influence the process being completed. Because there are several areas in the organization where weakness can be measured, this chapter focuses more on the supply chain and inventory control element of the organization. This text also addresses weaknesses in processes, management, and training of human resources. In the area of supply chain management, we will be looking at three fundamental parts: purchasing, suppliers/vendors, and inventory control.

Supply chain management operates much like the rest of the organization in that it is built on processes. Processes can be designed well or poorly and documented or not. Evaluating weak spots in supply chain management requires the manager to review the process and determine whether what has been designed is the most efficient and correct way to perform the tasks. This is an important step because it generally leads to a lesser-performing process or part of a process and reveals weak spots. Problems might be found within the processes themselves, or there might be issues not related to a process that result in its not being performed as desired. Weaknesses could also be found as a result of decision making by certain human resources. In supply chain management, there are many decisions that have to be made with regard to procurements, supplier or vendor relations, and inventory control. The ability of individuals to evaluate information and make sound decisions might be an area where weakness can be improved.

Procurements

The acquisition or purchase of supplies, materials, equipment, other resources, and inventory is generally performed by a procurements department. Within the procurement department, much like other departments in the organization, processes that control how procurements are carried out should be developed and documented. With any process evaluation or improvement exercise, managers must first sit down and review the documents to see how procurements have been designed to be performed. After careful review of the documents, it might be determined improvements can be made to eliminate weak areas or areas subject to fail.

Managers might solicit the help of the purchasing agents in the department to gather feedback on current processes they are performing and compare those to the current documents of those processes to see whether anything has changed. It might be revealed that purchasing agents are not following the documented process and this is why weaknesses or failure might occur. It also might reveal that the current process has been improved over the documented process, resulting in a more efficient way to perform the process. The manager might discover that there are processes that have not been designed, developed, or documented at all, and purchasing agents are simply performing activities on the fly with little or no guidance. This type of activity is where weakness or failure can be most prevalent. Depending on the skills and ability of the purchasing agents, weakness or strength is subject to the individual purchasing agent's ability. This is when a process can be out of control because the tasks and decisions that are carried out are at the discretion of the individual purchasing agent, which can result in inconsistency, success, or failure.

After the manager has reviewed the documentation and compared the process as documented against the processes as carried out by the purchasing agents, the manager might find that the purchasing agent's abilities play a larger role than expected in this particular capacity. This is when the manager should evaluate which purchasing agents have been assigned to specific tasks to ensure that their abilities, skills, and knowledge match what will be required in that process. In the procurement process, purchasing agents will find themselves having to make decisions that require a creative approach leading to an area of potential weakness or strength. When materials, equipment, resources, and inventory are purchased for an organization, things don't always go as planned and creative workaround strategies have to be developed. This might be the result of a phone call with a supplier who has informed you that something is no longer available and new action must be taken. This is when skill and experience come into play as to how the purchasing agent will approach the situation.

When filling a position in the organization, hiring managers must always evaluate the resource individually for their skills, background, and experience to ascertain whether an individual has the knowledge base to make critical decisions required in a position. In many cases, decisions might have to be made in the course of processes that are difficult to articulate in process documentation. This is again where strength or weakness might be seen on more of an individual basis. The manager has to separate what the process documentation calls for by design, for a particular situation, and discretionary decision making that the resource might have to conduct given a situation. In some cases, proper training can guide the resource as to on what basis certain decisions are made and what course of action is best for the situation. In other cases, experience might be the only way some decisions are made correctly because it would be difficult to document or train those types of decision scenarios. In either case, the human resource and the decision process are key to success and must be monitored by the manager.

Another area of strength or weakness within the procurement department is the ability to manage contractual agreements with suppliers and vendors. The relationship with the supplier is critical and can be an area of weakness if care is not taken in the development of the relationship. This relationship can be from informal occasional purchasing to complex contractual arrangements spanning years of deliveries and invoicing. In either case it's important to note that the relationship established with a supplier can and will generally be on two levels:

1. A relationship is *formally established between the organization and the supplier*, and in some cases they are engaged in a contractual agreement.

2. A relationship is established between the *actual buyer within the organization or the purchasing agent* in the procurement department *and the contact or contacts at the supplier.*

Relationships are formed between two people when repetitive purchasing is being done by the organization with a particular supplier, and that relationship can and might in some cases impact the outcome or success of certain procurements. With some organizations, orders received at a supplier are processed in a more structured way relative to pricing and any additional elements related to the objects being purchased. In some cases, special considerations might be taken with regard to pricing and priority shipping, and the person taking the order might have a physical inventory check done to ensure that product is shipped per the customer's requirements. This type of relationship is developed over long periods of time when a purchasing agent has several contacts with an order taker at the supplier and has developed a rapport.

Supplier Relationships

Supplier relationships can be a place where weaknesses can actually result in bigger problems for the organization. This can be in the form of higher prices, restock fees, not going the extra mile, and generally a lesser level of customer service by the supplier. This is not to suggest that forming the relationship should be done only to get perks out of your supplier; it is simply stating that the longer you do business with that supplier, the better relationship you have, and in some purchasing predicaments special consideration might be given by the supplier to help get something done. So it's best to cultivate and maintain good relationships with suppliers and vendors so as not to create problems or issues that could make future procurements difficult.

When things are purchased for the organization, they can be purchased under two primary categories:

1. Noncontractual direct purchases
2. Contractual purchases

Items purchased under a noncontractual purchase agreement are purchased over telephone, Internet, or mail-order types of order processing. These are considered simple orders, in which the purchasing agent has a particular item in mind and the supplier can fulfill delivery of the item with no special conditions. In most cases, noncontractual purchases fall under the supplier standard purchase agreement for pricing, delivery, payment, and return policy. Because most procurement would work fine under this type of an agreement, the supplier is not obligated to guarantee inventory levels, pricing, and special delivery or returns. If the procured item is not used on a product or sold by the organization, noncontractual purchase agreements for most items will be fine. For items purchased for products sold by the organization, projects or situations that might constitute special conditions, delivery schedules, or specifications, a contract might be a better way to control that type of procurement.

Power Tool

Contracts are used in purchasing to *clarify certain critical items* and to *guarantee certain conditions* called out in the contract that would be necessary by the organization.

If the organization is manufacturing products and the bill of material has been developed with material cost associated with it, this would be an example of items that would need to be purchased under contract to guarantee pricing and delivery schedules to maintain the overall cost of an item being manufactured. Contracts can also be used to help protect the organization, and if weaknesses are discovered with certain supplier relationships, contracts are a way to help strengthen the procurement process.

Power Tool

Contracts can be negotiated by those skilled in negotiating to help set *conditions for procurements* and eliminate weaker negotiating that might happen periodically in the department.

This will be the case only if the organization has resources skilled in negotiating contracts. If contracts are not negotiated correctly, weaknesses in the procurement department—such as poor price negotiation or poor delivery schedules—can become permanent and long-term problems can be locked into the contract. It's important, if contracts are to be used, that resources skilled in contracts carry out this process to ensure the best interest of the organization.

Weakness can also be seen within the information that procurement departments use to make purchases. Information is powerful when used correctly, but can be devastating if incomplete or incorrect. Purchasing agents can procure the correct item only if they have all the pertinent information at hand to ensure that the item meets all the requirements requested. All too often, items are purchased with partial or incorrect information and, to the disappointment of those requesting the purchase, upon delivery they find that something is not right and the purchase has to be redone. This weakness results in wasted time and money for both the organization and the supplier and is something that can be improved or eliminated through process improvement. The procurement department can develop tools that better organize information such as order request forms to help structure and outline a minimum amount of information required to make a purchase. Developing these types of tools improves the procurement process and helps eliminate incorrect purchases due to lack of information.

Another form of information relates to supporting documentation with regard to purchasing. This might be a bill of materials, or a revision of drawings such as a mechanical drawing revision that would indicate the most recent changes or modifications to the item. Changes within the organization are inevitable, but they have to go through a process in which they are documented so that others in the organization will have the latest information about that particular item. If something is being procured off of a mechanical drawing or a bill of materials, it's important for the latest revision to be purchased so as not to continue purchasing items from an older revision that's no longer wanted. This is another example in which a structured change order process can reduce mistakes and weaknesses within the organization.

Suppliers

Now that we have looked at some areas of potential weakness within the organization, it's time to look outside the organization to the suppliers and vendors the organization does business with. Suppliers, as organizations themselves, also have processes they have developed in selling product, and they are generally expected to follow those processes. As we have seen in some situations, based on the relationship between the two organizations, some special considerations can be made that improve the situation for either side, but in most cases the supplier is following a particular order process that has been established. There can be several weaknesses in a supplier relationship that can be avoided:

1. New versus established supplier
2. Manufacturer versus distributor
3. Internet based
4. Domestic or foreign

How long a supplier has been in business can play a role in the relationship with that supplier and in whether it is a weakness or strength. Older, more established suppliers have more experience and might be less likely to make basic fundamental mistakes in order processing. Because this is the general perception with older companies, it should be proven through the relationship and not simply accepted as the rule. Newer companies might or might not have well-established processes and might have lesser-experienced people who make the relationship more problematic. As with the older companies, this is simply a perception to take note of, and it should be verified through the relationship and not established as a rule. On the other hand, older companies might have a tendency to be more set in their ways and less likely to be aggressive and negotiate for business. Newer companies wanting to take market share might be more aggressive, putting them at a slightly better competitive advantage.

Power Tool

It is always best to *do a little research on the company you are looking to do business with* to get some background information. Start with *one or two small purchases* to test their process and abilities to *determine how a future relationship might look.*

Suppliers fall into two categories: manufacturers and distributors. Manufacturers of products in some cases might sell and distribute their own product directly. Other manufacturers might choose to have their products distributed by secondary companies called distributors. Distributors in most cases do not manufacture anything but simply purchase product for resale. A distributor might play a small role in some assembly of items they distribute, but this would not be considered manufacturing but rather just offering products they sell in an assembled form. Weaknesses can be found with both manufacturers and distributors.

Manufacturers that sell their own products have a tendency to focus on the processes within production and less on product distribution and sales. If they have not developed processes to organize sales, this can make it difficult from a procurement standpoint to do business with them. If the manufacturer produces a simpler product, more emphasis might be placed on developing distribution and sales that allows the manufacturer to compete against both distributors and other manufacturers who distribute their own product. The strength in working with a manufacturer is that they have more resources to help with product knowledge and questions concerning particular product details. The weaknesses typically are an underdeveloped order-processing department that makes procurements with that company slightly more difficult. A distributor's weakness generally is in a lack of product knowledge or information because they typically do most of their work out of manufacturers' catalogs. Distributors also find it difficult to manage returns and/or perform warranty work. Distributors typically have a well-developed order-processing department because that is their primary function.

Organizations in this day and age have found Internet-based business or e-commerce to be an improvement in the overall business strategy. This can be a plus for the procurements department or those trying to find information on product and pricing because the Internet can facilitate quick and easy search and information gathering, meaning less time spent on phone calls with companies. Older, more established companies in some cases have not developed an Internet-based presence like a Web site, catalogs, and/or order-processing capability. If the company does not have an Internet presence, they will have to conduct their business through hard-bound catalogs or CD-based catalogs, as well as phone call, e-mail, or mail-order processing. This is old-school and was done for decades; it's not that it's wrong, but it's just another way to reduce competitive advantage and lose market share.

Power Tool

The Internet can give organizations the ability to *be seen around the world,* and to tell the *history* and *structure* of the organization as well as telling about the *products, pricing, and order capabilities.*

Purchasing agents need information such as corporate headquarters' location, branch location addresses, and phone numbers that allow them to get in contact with the organization. This can be a big competitive advantage over companies that have no Internet presence. A weakness with companies that have no Internet presence is the increased difficulty purchasing agents have in finding information about the company. This can be a problem for the purchasing agent, because it usually takes much longer and requires more work to verify company information.

Companies in either manufacturing or distribution generally find it easier to work with companies closer to their location. This is primarily due to the price and logistics of shipping. Domestic companies typically do not have the issues with shipping and customs that foreign companies might run into. This can be a weakness, but as more foreign companies are doing business with other countries around the world, shipping and customs are becoming a more streamlined process and are not always seen necessarily as a weakness. If foreign countries do not have personnel who can speak the same language as those in your organization, this can typically be where weakness is found. As you have seen, information accuracy in the procurement process is very important and the language barrier can present issues with information accuracy.

Power Tool

Care must be taken in doing business *with organizations in foreign countries* to make sure that the *contact person* the procurement agent will be dealing with is *well-versed in the language and that the lines of communication are clear.*

Inventory Control

One area in supply chain management that organizations might struggle with is inventory control. Depending on the size and type of the organization, inventory can be a relatively simple element to solve or can be very complex. If the organization is involved in manufacturing, inventory will be at three levels:

1. Incoming inspection of materials received—Materials for manufacturing that are first received and inspected.

2. Materials needed to manufacture the product—Inventory purchased for product, stored at the facility, and/or located within manufacturing referred to as work in process (WIP).

3. Finished goods inventory ready for shipment—Product completed through manufacturing and ready for shipment.

Incoming Inspection

Inventory is typically purchased for manufactured items based on specifications, and when received, it is verified against the specification, bill material, purchase order, or drawings through an incoming inspection process. The skills and experience, as well as training, of the incoming inspection staff are critical to correctly receiving product from suppliers. This is the first point of contact with material from suppliers that allows the organization to accept or reject nonconforming product. All too often, weaknesses in incoming inspection allow nonconforming material to pass through to the production floor, resulting in damaged goods, failure, and rework that costs the organization time and money. This is usually a result of poor or no process development, or resources with insufficient skill or training. The incoming inspection process is the gate of material receiving and should be taken seriously because this can be a big source of weakness.

Power Tool

Properly trained incoming inspection staff can *save the company time* in blocking nonconforming material *and money* in avoiding rework on the production floor.

Work in Process (WIP)

Production floors can be busy environments with machines, benches, conveyers, carts, and human resources everywhere. Although production environments can look like chaos, there is a difference between no logical meaning to the layout and a well-defined purpose to it that just gives the appearance of being unorganized. One area of concern in designing production floors is when inventory is scattered all throughout the production floor and very easily can present a tracking problem. Weaknesses typically can be found on the production floor in the following areas:

- Managing inventory without damaging it
- Locating inventory sensibly so that it can be quickly and easily accessed by manufacturing staff
- Managing nonconforming material or rework

Production inventory accountability is one of the hardest things to manage because inventory is moving constantly through various processes and can be challenging to keep track of. The manager might solicit the help of process developers or manufacturing engineers to address WIP inventory and evaluate weak spots on the production floor. The first potential problem area is how inventory is stored. Depending on what type of inventory there is, this can be simple or can require complex shelves and racking systems with elaborate holding and separation methodologies. Weakness is evident when inventory can be damaged simply by the way it is stored and can cause rework or scrap as well as costing resource time.

Power Tool

Inventory management systems that are *designed for the product* are an example of Streamline Thinking and *protect material and human resource time and costs.*

The second potential problem area is in the placement of material and inventory at the process work spaces. One of the most costly expenses is human resource efficiency, relating to the number of movements workers have to make during a process. Evaluating where the materials and inventory are in relation to the person performing the process can reveal weaknesses if the inventory is not optimized in its placement. Remedying the situation might require using better racks, bins, or shelving, or might involve a change in the layout of a work space that reduces how far the person has to reach or walk during the process. This can be a big time saver and can eliminate weakness in resource efficiency and production floor space.

The third potential problem area is in managing nonconforming inventory and rework. It is a known fact that in most production environments, there will be damaged goods, rework, or scrap that will need to be accounted for. This presents two things to consider: tracking the material and where to store the material during evaluation. This again might be an opportunity for a process developer or manufacturing engineer to identify an area in production to manage the process of rework evaluation. Tracking the material can become difficult because the inventory might be taken apart and now stored in pieces, mislabeled and confused with other good inventory, or just lost in the system somehow.

Power Tool

How the material is stored can play a role in reducing this confusion, and better design of this type of process allows special tracking, storage, and segregation of product to *isolate nonconforming materials* from the rest of production.

This area within production can be a resource drain on the organization, but if properly designed and managed, it can save the organization from this potentially large weakness.

Finished Goods Inventory

Finally, finished goods inventory or manufactured product that is ready for shipment can sometimes be an area of weakness. This area, although more highly controlled than the other two areas, can have the same cost and schedule impact on the organization due to damaged goods and inaccurate shipping counts. When manufactured products are finished and ready for shipment, it's important to ensure that the product is stored in a condition such that it will not be damaged. In most cases products are shipped in some form of packaging or container that protect the item in shipping. This can again be an area of weakness that can easily get overlooked; much work was invested in the design of the product and the manufacturing, but the product still has to be successfully stored and shipped. This will generate an evaluation of both the packaging used for the product and the shipping receiving area, as well as storage and the general handling of the product. Another potential weakness is with the accountability of the finished product and, if product is damaged in storage or shipping areas, how is it tracked to rework.

Supply chain management can be very complex for an organization, but that doesn't mean it has to be full of problems and potential weakness. Even the most complex organizations can have well-thought-out supply chain and inventory management systems that are very efficient and run very smoothly. This could come about in part because managers determined that they could not manage that part of the organization, at that size, and be cost-effective. So they developed a plan to break the organization into functional areas and evaluate critical areas for potential risk and weakness. It is not that hard, and when improvements are made, the benefits are seen and can be measured for success. This will generate more interest in this type of process improvement as the manager starts to feel that she has more control over elements of the supply chain.

Power Tool

As improvements to weaknesses result in *improved cost and time management,* other *managers will get onboard* and implement the same thinking, which helps *improve the entire organization.*

Power Tool Summary

- Contracts are used in purchasing to *clarify certain critical items* and to *guarantee certain condition* called out in the contract that would be necessary by the organization.

- *Contracts can be negotiated* by those skilled in negotiating to help set *conditions for procurements* and eliminate weaker negotiating that might happen periodically in the department.

- It is always best to *do a little research on the company you are looking to do business with* to get some background information. Start with *one or two small purchases* to test their process and abilities to *determine how a future relationship might look.*

- *The Internet* can give organizations the ability to *be seen around the world,* and to tell the *history* and *structure* of the organization as well as telling about the *products, pricing, and order capabilities.*

- *Care must be taken* in doing business *with organizations in foreign countries* to make sure that the *contact person* the procurement agent will be dealing with is *well-versed in the language and that the lines of communication are clear.*

- *Properly trained* incoming inspection staff can *save the company time* in blocking nonconforming material *and money* in avoiding rework on the production floor.

- Inventory management systems that are *designed for the product* are an example of Streamline Thinking, and *protect material and human resource time and costs.*

- *How the material is stored* can play a role in reducing this confusion, and better design of this type of process allows special tracking, storage, and segregation of product to *isolate nonconforming materials* from the rest of production.

- As improvements to weaknesses result in *improved cost and time management,* other *managers will get onboard* and implement the same thinking, which helps *improve the entire organization.*

11

Organizing for Efficiency

When organizations look at cost reduction, the focus can typically be on elimination, which usually points to human resources. This can be a result of paradigms or the mind-set of managers who are used to looking at cost reduction in the form of elimination. Although eliminating things can reduce cost, it's the approach taken that can be improved to optimize what needs to be eliminated, if anything, to accomplish the goal. Project managers using Streamline Thinking have to look at their project from an organizational standpoint. Organization represents a process that results in efficiency, not necessarily elimination. It's important for the manager to understand the concept of organization and what options and alternatives it can present within the department.

Because the process of being organized starts with the correct mind-set, we have to understand what being organized actually is. Organization is a process that requires Streamline Thinking; you will need to visualize the goal and then sequence the steps to accomplish that goal. Streamline Thinking takes the steps that are actually needed, evaluates the resources needed at each step, and aligns or groups those resources to be most efficient. Organization is very similar; it looks to sequencing or compartmentalizing things to better organize them. This thought process can be utilized in several ways: organization of thoughts, approach to performing a job, organization of immediate work spaces, and organization of the department. Evaluating what is needed at each step, grouping or compartmentalizing, and better sequencing for efficiency is thinking in the form of a process.

When organization is understood as a process, it can then be used like a process to accomplish an objective. The manager develops this process by generating a list of steps (tasks) he will use in evaluating how organized the department actually is. If cost reduction is an objective, using an organizational approach will have the manager focused on *what* they have, *when,* and *why* it's used versus how many they have and how many they can eliminate. This approach requires the manager to analyze his department in terms of being organized, such as evaluating work-space efficiency and capital equipment placement, as well as human resource assignments. This organizational approach can be used at all levels within the organization and can be applied to most functional areas within the organization. It is also important to understand that organization starts as a mind-set, so the manager must first practice organizing his thoughts and how he approaches his job.

Power Tool

Thinking in terms of *what, when,* and *why,* rather than in terms of *how many,* forces the manager to evaluate the department as processes, not just work being done and numbers of human resources.

Power Tool

When managers start *thinking from an organized perspective* using Streamline Thinking, this allows the manager to *look at the department and the resources from an organized viewpoint.*

When organizing becomes a process, it can then be understood by others in the organization and become a part of the culture of that organization. This is no easy task, because some managers might see the value in being organized, whereas other managers simply do not have an organized mind and see it as being difficult and meaning more work in managing their responsibilities. The best way for a manager to communicate the value of organizing is by example. This can start with the organization of the manager's own department and the culture of organizing developed within that department.

Power Tool

The *benefits of a department being organized* will be seen by other departments and managers, *validating organization as a process* in not only streamlining the department, but in process improvement.

At What Level Should Organizing Be Done?

When you're analyzing how to best implement organization, it's good to understand that this can be at three primary levels within the organization:

1. **High-level**—Executive-level management having oversight of the organization
2. **Midlevel**—Midlevel management departmental oversight
3. **Low-level**—Immediate work areas

High-level

As with other process implementation efforts, the best results are realized when top-down acceptance is seen by all in the organization. When mid- and lower-level management and others in the organization see the buy-in of executive management, this validates and brings credibility to what's being implemented. Executive-level management can look at organization from the perspective of how the business is divided up, what business they are in, what products are manufactured and sold, and what location or use of facilities they have chosen. Organizing at this level is best done at the beginning or start of an organization or a company, but in most cases can be reviewed by executive-level management at any time during the organization's existence. This is not a new concept to executive-level management; many organizations have been restructured or reorganized throughout history. This can be the result of downsizing efforts, changes in strategic objectives, or expansion of organizations including acquisitions. In these cases, executives are making changes based on business necessity, which might or might not include improving efficiency. The real question here is why these evaluations are being made and what approach should be taken to make changes.

When executives look at reorganizing from an efficiency standpoint, it will require a clear understanding of the goal and a Streamline Thinking approach. It can sometimes be difficult for executive management to step away from cost-reduction thinking, because this usually causes them to evaluate reductions in staff or equipment.

Power Tool

The key for executive-level management is to *think about organizing for efficiency,* which might simply mean *reorganizing what they already have,* which *might or might not include eliminating.*

To better illustrate this concept, we can look at an example of a used-car lot. The owner of a used-car lot studies many vehicles and makes purchases based on market demand, but might not be selling the vehicles as quickly as expected. As the market research shows, the dealer has the correct vehicles in stock and the pricing is competitive—so what is causing this problem? Marketing is sometimes a key element and the approach might be to look at the placement of the vehicles on the lot. This requires the dealer to step away from elimination thinking (taking the "nonselling" vehicles back to the auction), but leads him to look at the "organization" of vehicles that he currently has. Grouping certain vehicles together, say, all the trucks in one area, sedans in another area, and sports cars in one area, allows the customers to compare like vehicles in one particular area of the car lot. They can then evaluate models, colors, options, and pricing much more easily and see better deals more quickly. This did not require the dealer to eliminate any vehicles, just simply rearrange the inventory he already had. It might be determined that placing key vehicles in the front of the dealership during certain seasons of the year allows interested customers to spot those vehicles more quickly on the lot.

Power Tool

This is *organizational thinking,* which has you *focusing on the structure* of the layout for customer efficiency *and not elimination* and cost reduction for efficiency.

This type of thinking can be applied to the business strategy in determining how many of what type facilities are being used, or possibly where facilities are located in proximity to suppliers and/or customers and raw materials. Executives have the power to make changes if a better-organized plan results in efficiency. A net result of becoming more efficient will generally, in time, result in better use of resources and cost reductions.

Midlevel

The same thought process holds true for midlevel managers in understanding the difference between the reorganization for efficiency and reductions and elimination for efficiency. Managers will also have to express acceptance of this concept so that others in their department will buy-in to this process. Others in the department will need to see that the manager is convinced that this approach can work or the lack of effort will make realizing success difficult. We can use the same example of the car dealership with the midlevel manager being responsible for the service area and mechanics bays.

This is considered a department within the dealership, and the manager has the responsibility of making the most efficient use of the space. For changes in efficiency, the manager needs to shift the thought process of reduction or elimination to simply reorganization. This might involve looking at the layout of the mechanics area and better grouping job functions, say, having oil changes in one area, tire replacement and rotation in another area, and the mechanics service bays grouped in a separate area. In better organizing these areas, the mechanics will have only the tools and service equipment needed for the type of task designed to be carried out in that area. This process did not eliminate anything, but just better organized the areas for efficiency, allowing the mechanics to focus on the type of service they are assigned. This can reveal unutilized space that can now be used for something else or possibly open the door for other types of services previously not offered.

This organizational thinking can be applied for midlevel managers within business by having them evaluate their particular department for best use of human resources, capital equipment, and facility space.

Power Tool

Midlevel managers can self-train this type of thinking by *creating a challenge:*

- Cost reduction being limited only to reorganization
- No reduction or elimination allowed

Organizational thinking will force the manager to make necessary improvements in better organization that will produce a more cost-effective way to run the department. The manager has to look at layouts, work space, human resource traffic patterns, and so on to accomplish this type of improvement. This can also be a way managers can train their thought process to follow organized streamline thinking, thus stepping away from reduction-and-elimination-type thinking.

Low-level

Being organized within a particular work space is every bit as important as midlevel and high-level organization because it can yield the same type of results. Work-space organization can generally be accomplished in two ways:

1. **Task worker input**—This is where the task worker in a particular work area takes responsibility for the organization of that area. If the manager feels it's appropriate, she can empower the worker to evaluate the area to see whether a better layout of their work space would be more efficient. This allows the worker to take ownership of the work space and allows the worker to be creative in making efficient changes. The resources directly involved with the process have the best ideas to make it more efficient because they have to work with the inefficiencies every day. Any changes to the work area should be reviewed by a manager for approval and to validate that the changes are justified and do result in a better-organized work space. This also allows the workers to be involved in the organizing plan that the overall company is trying to initiate.

2. **Process or Manufacturing Engineer input**—If the organization has process or manufacturing engineering resources, it might be the decision of the manager to utilize these resources to evaluate work space. Process and manufacturing engineers typically are resources assigned to design work-space areas and evaluate those areas with efficiency and organization in mind. These resources many times will look at a work space slightly different than the task worker or the manager because they are

looking at work space from a process standpoint. Task workers are "normalized," or used to the work space, and they can't see inefficiency and wouldn't want to change if they had to. In other cases, task workers might show reluctance in making improvements because they simply don't like change! There might be occasions when manufacturing engineers want to work in conjunction with task workers to gain their input for problems or issues they want to solve in reorganizing the work space. This again focuses on the organization of work-space materials, equipment, and human resource movement, and not reduction or elimination.

The low-level evaluation of work space can have very promising outcomes because organization can be at a simpler level and quickly accomplished. This might reveal things that are no longer necessary in the process that can be eliminated, but the focus is on reorganization for efficiency and optimization of a work space. Examples of organization considerations might include the following:

1. **Placement of certain tools or materials**—This includes how they are positioned, binned, and located in proximity to the task worker.

2. **Sequence of how a process takes place to optimize the movement of the task worker**—Movements that a task worker makes require energy and time, and optimizing the placement of items for the worker reduces the amount of movement and therefore time it takes to perform the process.

3. **Placement of computer programs and files that workers will need to access to perform their jobs**—If programs or files are not organized well within a network system, this can result in time spent searching for things that workers need in order to perform their tasks. Organizing things on the network or consolidating them into functional areas of a network can help the worker access and utilize programs and files more efficiently and therefore save time.

The manager must realize that, at this level, even the smallest change can make a difference, especially if it is something performed several times. Small changes do add up over an entire department and organization. This is also good training for staff to have an organized mind-set in how they think, as well as how they approach their jobs. This type of training pays off in the long run as streamline, organized thinking by large portions of the organization results in large numbers of resources paying more attention to the details, which results in efficiency and cost reductions at all levels. This is also how management can make reductions in cost, but not always through reductions in staff.

Power Tool

Training management and staff at all levels in *being better organized* is really about creating a smarter work force that will prove the value of this approach every day by incremental organizational efforts.

Design It In

So part of what we're looking at in organizational thinking is in the mind-set and how we view something, and also in how things are physically arranged or sequenced, but this needs to go a step further and be designed in as well. When processes and work spaces are first designed, they are supposed to be designed in the most efficient manner from the start. After work has begun and as it continues over long periods, a work space can start to change. The task worker might begin moving things around or extra, unneeded things might begin to accumulate in the work space. This activity is not the fault of any particular person, but simply the unconscious act of migrating away from optimum organization. *(This can also be avoided when organizational thinking is trained and used by the staff.)*

Companies, departments, and work space should have organization as a top priority when they are first created, but if they already exist, they should still be evaluated for optimization in how they are organized. When processes performed within a department are first created, organization should be designed in from the beginning, but this needs to be the mind-set of the person designing the process. Resources who have creative and organized approaches to process development will typically see and design in organization as they develop a process. Being able to visualize organization at the start allows the process to be developed from that basis. This is why it's important to have resources who understand and can implement this type of approach, because most in the company will not think this way. Resources who already design processes with organization will be best, but other resources might have to be trained and might need practice.

Power Tool

The important element when you are designing organization into a process is to remember Streamline Thinking, *having only what's required for the process,* and considering how the process is *laid out for most efficient use of space and movement of the resources.*

Cost Benefit

When organization is implemented, in most cases, this will result in improved efficiency, which can equate to cost savings. Improved efficiency can lead to other benefits for the company, such as improved use of capital equipment and materials, facility space, and use of human resources. When we evaluate efficiency, using organization, it's important to remember that we are looking at the optimization of resources, not necessarily the reduction or elimination of resources. For example, if two processes require the same piece of equipment or materials, it might be better to locate these processes next to each other so that the movement of human resources is reduced and sharing of equipment or materials can be accomplished. In some cases, the consolidation of two processes might result in several outcomes, including optimized use of equipment, facility space, and human resources. If the company has to purchase certain pieces of equipment or materials, it is generally based on the requirements within the process. If the process is designed with an eye to organization, this will result in a cost savings and having to supply fewer equipment materials initially.

When equipment and materials have to be researched, purchased, and then received, these will require human resource time that can be used for other things. If fewer items have to be purchased as a result of optimized processes, this reduces not only what has to be purchased, but the time it takes to purchase. Organizing a process or department is about Streamline Thinking that will ultimately connect several areas within the operation. When the operation is more organized and efficient, other areas benefit as well. Being organized starts with the individual and results in organized behavior. This behavior produces organized work, which results in a more efficient operation, saving time and money!

Power Tool Summary

- Thinking in terms of *what, when,* and *why,* rather than in terms of *how many,* forces the manager to evaluate the department as processes, not just work being done and numbers of human resources.

- When managers start thinking *from an organized perspective* using Streamline Thinking, this allows the manager to *look at the department and the resources from an organized viewpoint.*

- The *benefits of a department being organized* will be seen by other departments and managers, *validating organization as a process* in not only streamlining the department but in process improvement.

- The key for executive-level management is to *think about organizing for efficiency*, which might simply mean *reorganizing what they already have*, which *might or might not include eliminating.*

- This is *organizational thinking,* which has you *focusing on the structure* of the layout for customer efficiency *and not elimination* and cost reduction for efficiency.

- Midlevel managers can self-train this type of thinking by *creating a challenge*:

  - Cost reduction being limited only to reorganization

  - No reduction or elimination allowed

- *Training management and staff* at all levels in *being better organized* is really about creating a smarter work force that will prove the value of this approach every day by incremental organizational efforts.

- The important element when you are designing organization into a process is to remember Streamline Thinking, *having only what's required for the process,* and considering how the process is *laid out for most efficient use of space and movement of the resources.*

12

Managing Change

Every organization needs to continually evaluate its business environment, market, and competitors to validate the overall strategic objective of the organization. This evaluation can show that the organization is structured and performing correctly to meet business objectives, or it can indicate that improvements need to be made to better align with the strategic objective. When an organization is faced with the reality of having to make significant changes, that can create high levels of stress within management.

In evaluating sustainable success, organizations fall into two categories: those that have well-established structure that meets the strategic objective requiring little or no significant change, and those that require significant change to realign with the strategic objective. This should not be a comparison of older companies versus newer companies, or larger versus smaller, but rather an evaluation of how well management has maintained the operation and kept it aligned with the strategic objective. Older companies might have made significant changes early on and, given their market, can stay aligned with the strategic objective without further significant change. On the other hand, it is the older organizations which might realize that change is required in order to stay competitive within their market, imposing a higher stress on management.

Newer organizations can fall under the same two categories. Starting off new, they might have been able to align themselves within their market, be competitive, and have a well-established structure that met the strategic objective. These newer companies can also find they need to make incremental improvements as they mature in the market in order to stay competitive, also imposing stress on their management. One thing remains for most organizations: Change is inevitable at some point. The question is, how prepared is the organization to make significant changes?

This is the make-or-break point for organizations because change, although well intended, can result in damage or devastation for an organization. This should then put the ball back into the court of management asking why we are making the change. When organizations evaluate the reality of having to make significant changes, they should attempt to do this only if they have a well-established process for making change. Change without data, planning, structured approach, and a measurement system leaves management typically focusing on what the change will need to be instead of planning and implementing a change to ensure the desired outcome. Change should be viewed as a systematic approach to improving the organization rather than being a daunting, risk-intensive gamble.

Why Change Anything?

Organizations look at the need for change from different perspectives, which might include success with strategic positioning within the marketplace, general efficiencies, and profitability within the organization, as well as the general nature of business. Change is not always necessary but must be justified through the use of measurement, the gathering of data, and the comparison of data against the intended strategic objective. Some organizations might avoid significant change due to a lack of resources capable of managing change or to avoid significant risk associated with change. Most significant change within an organization stems from an evaluation of the organization's position and success within the marketplace.

Market Position

Some organizations, based on the view of executive management, are content with the way the organization has positioned itself within a marketplace and do not feel the need to change. Although this might appear to be acceptable, this can be a result of opinion or perception and not actual data. The only way executive management will know that they are meeting strategic objectives and being successful in their market is by reviewing the data. It is the data that would then suggest that change is justified, therefore calling for a plan of action.

Products and Profit

Organizations might find that they are well positioned in their marketplace but might find it difficult to maintain desired profitability. This might be as a result of product mix and competitive pricing, but might point to improvements that can be made to increase profit margins or reduce operating overhead. These types of changes, in most cases, are at midlevel management and are generally process-oriented.

As you have already seen, processes are very important in the organization, and improvements can be evaluated in several ways. Smaller changes can be made in areas of engineering, manufacturing, shipping and receiving, inventory control, and supply chain management, as well as human resources and administration departments. Products and organization manufacturers can also undergo improvements in the materials used, as well as the processes to create the product. These improvements can result in better profit margin for the product as well as reduced overhead costs in producing the product.

Better Technology

Change can be in the general nature of doing business and in the role technology can play in conducting business. When an organization is profitable and successful in accomplishing its strategic objective, management can fall into a comfort zone, at which point anything suggested to upset this balance typically is seen as not necessary and is rejected. Technology, throughout the years, has presented industry with new and more efficient ways to accomplish business processes. Managers, even if they are comfortable in the success of their business, need to review new techniques that might allow the organization to improve its efficiency, profitability, and overhead costs.

Management must also realize that if new and improved techniques are available on the market, their competitors might also be evaluating these techniques to make improvements.

If competitors can make incremental improvements to overhead costs and efficiencies, this gives them a competitive advantage in the marketplace because they can lower prices or offer services at a reduced rate. This will then put added pressure on the organization, and typically this is how organizations lose their position incrementally over time in a marketplace. It is imperative that members of management continually seek improvements and make changes because their competitors will be doing the same.

Problems with Change

When managers ask why a change should be made, this is a result of four fundamental concerns surrounding the process of change:

1. People don't like change.
2. Change involves risk.
3. There might be a lack of data.
4. Investment is required.

Executive and midlevel managers, as well as most of the workforce, find themselves battling an element of human nature that simply does not like change! This is due primarily to problems associated with change. This can be as a result of the type of change being made, because some changes are easier than others for a manager to implement. This can also be a result of not having a well-defined process for making change within the organization. Not having an established change process within an organization leaves managers to implement a change with little or no guidance as to important steps required to make a change successful. Managers inherently do not want to fail, so they avoid change.

People Don't Like Change

As already noted, one of the first hurdles to get over in evaluating change is the simple fact that human nature does not like change. Most people in management, as well as the workforce, like it when things for which they are responsible are going well because this provides them a level of contentment, security, and self-confidence. Although this is typically the goal, managers should constantly review their processes to ensure that they are being conducted correctly and to evaluate any new improvements that could be made. Part of the reason people do not like change is fear of the unknown, and the risk associated with something that might not go as planned. These feelings are welcome because it is the byproduct of our internal check system to question change. This is good, but it needs to be answered with having an organized and structured change process that can validate why and how a change can be implemented.

Power Tool

When people see the *positive result* of an organized change-control process, they are *more comfortable with participating in change*!

Change Involves Risk

One of the biggest concerns with change involves the potential risks that might be associated with any level of change. As you have seen, risks are inevitable but should not steer the manager away from change, because risk can be identified and planned for. Risk does address the world of the unknown, but surprisingly, there is more known about the risks associated with change than one might think.

In developing the plan for a change, each step in the change process can be evaluated for problems. Potential problems can be identified and contingencies can be planned to address those problems if they do occur. Project managers use this tool to map their way through a project and plan for problems before they occur. When risks are identified and contingency efforts planned, this can reduce the stress associated with change because it reduces the unknown elements. Risks can then be a part of the change plan and will have visibility, eliminating many unknown parts of the change.

There Might Be a Lack of Data

An important process that organizations should develop is evaluating and analyzing data to base decisions on. Some decisions within the organization are made by executive and midlevel managers simply based on emotion or opinion. Decisions have been made by organizations for decades based on emotion and opinion that did actually have a positive outcome. If we were to go back and really analyze decisions that look as though they were made based on feeling or opinion, we might find that the opinion was actually based on some level of knowledge an executive had that simply appeared to be opinion. If there was no data to justify a decision, the decision would be seen more as a gamble, having much higher levels of risk associated with it.

Managers should strive to make their decisions based on actual data so that the basis is justified by real conditions and not simply on opinion or emotion. Although this data justifies a course of action, it simply justifies the action and not the means or the path to implement that action. Data will also suggest what type of change, or how much change, might be required.

Power Tool

Knowing the real data associated with a proposed change *helps managers be more confident* in why changes are made and what the desired outcomes should be.

Data also allows for a measurement system that, after a change has been implemented, validates the success of the change and the sustainability of that change.

Investment Is Required

Organizations constantly have to evaluate investments made to carry out the strategic objective. Investments might include the acquisition of facilities, capital equipment, and human resources, but don't always include investments needed for change within the organization. If a significant change has to be evaluated by executive management, an important problem with this change will be understating the investment required. Although executives might agree on the need for a change to be made, the bigger argument might result from the investment needed to implement the change. Investments required to implement change also have risk associated with them. Investments might include allocation of human resources taken away from their normal duties, use of capital equipment, and use of cash flow or lines of credit required to implement the change. Designing the implementation of change will take time, resources, and careful evaluation of what resources are required (investment) and will be available when needed.

Executive and midlevel management must understand the inherent problems surrounding change, such as human nature and rejection of change, associated risks, lack of data to justify change, and the overall investment required to implement change. Although these are real problems, they can be minimized, depending on the type of change, if a change process is in place to organize the implementation process.

Types of Change

Executive and midlevel management might find that change can be required at all levels within the organization. Managers might also find that some change is approved while other change is rejected based on the type of change being proposed. The type of change will also play a large role in the amount of resources the organization will expand to implement a proposed change. In most cases, the benefit of a proposed change is directly proportional to the type of change being made.

This is an important aspect of change because the goal or benefit of a proposed change should be balanced with the time and resources required to make that change. Changes are then cost-effective if the outcome produces an improvement capable of paying back the implementation cost, as well as sustainable benefit. Therefore, the type of change becomes important because it will dictate the level of investment by the organization, as well as the risk and potential outcome expected from that change. There are several types of changes that organizations can evaluate, such as organizational structure, type of business and product mix, processes, policies, and documentation. The type of change being proposed might also dictate the approval process that will be required, and which people will be involved in evaluating the change.

Organizational Structure

Organizations are structured based on several different aspects of business, which can include the size of the organization, how many facilities are required, and different types of business the organization has. Within this organizational structure, operations typically have an executive management structure, a midlevel management structure, and sometimes a lower-level management depending on the size of the organization. Changes within this organizational structure vary in complexity—depending on the level within the organization. For instance, changing members of the Board of Directors or officers within the corporation might be slightly harder than changing the manager of a department or a supervisor of a production line.

This type of change is very important and must also go through a change process to ensure that all the required steps have been accounted for and will be carried out correctly. This process also includes data that will establish the criteria for a position and will be used for evaluating candidates for that position. It might be evaluating the current structure and positions to validate managerial effectiveness. This might include the addition of midlevel managers to better oversee departments within an organization. This might also require the reduction of levels of management to better consolidate the management structure. These types of changes have to be evaluated, like any other change, as to the cost benefit. When management personnel are added, does the increased overhead cost benefit the organization, or does this simply add another management position? These types of changes can be difficult to quantify with real cost-saving numbers. This type of decision might be qualified based on current resource allocation and comments from other management staff who are overworked.

Changes to organizational structure that typically include additions, reductions, or consolidation can also include reassignment within management. This type of change evaluates the skill set of an individual manager who might be better utilized in a different managerial position. This type of change benefits the organization with better use of current resources, not requiring the addition of management resources or the ongoing underutilization of current resources.

Type of Business

Organizations start with the strategic objective in mind, but as market conditions can change, so the organization might have to respond to those changes. This might be the result of a market completely going away, requiring the organization to respond with a new strategic goal and objective for a different market. If an organization determines that it will participate in a completely different market, this will require significant change at all levels within the organization. If the organization is monitoring mild shifts in type or quantity of products, this might require the organization to make only slight changes in its product type or production capabilities.

Some organizations that are successful in one particular market might find an opportunity to be involved in a second and completely different market at the same time. This might require the organization to create separate fundamental business units, which require the organization to be restructured accordingly. Although this could be seen as significant change, executive management can still develop a process to evaluate and implement this level of change.

No matter what change to the organization is being evaluated, whether it be a complete retooling for a completely different market, simply adding new product, or adding other business units through expansion or acquisition, it still requires a *process* for change. This type of change also requires data that will need to be collected and evaluated for a change in the business strategic objective. Change will also have risk associated with it, as well as investment required to implement the change that will also be part of the *change process* and may be required at any level within the organization.

Power Tool

It's the *development of the change process* that will help organize the components required in managing the implementation of change and ensure the success of change.

Process Changes

On a smaller scale, changes that happen on a regular basis have the same components of change that have to be managed in the change process. Processes are those systematic groupings of tasks that the organization carries out to achieve the strategic objective. As important as change is at the executive level in structuring the organization, changes to the organization's processes should be seen as equally important. Processes are developed with a goal in mind and, as you have seen, can be evaluated for highest efficiency, use of resources, elimination of waste, and organization to most effectively accomplish the goal. Therefore, changes should be made only through measuring areas of the process and finding that something can be improved. The change process should then be followed to help standardize how processes are evaluated, changed, and measured to validate the change. This is also how organizations can control changes being made to processes throughout the organization.

Policy Changes

Organizations establish policies that manage various elements of the organization. This can be how business is conducted, how human resources are controlled, how safety is managed, and how certain accounting practices are controlled. Changes in policies have their own level of complexity, risk, and impact to the organization that have to be considered before change can be implemented.

Policies controlling human resource activities and conduct can have severe impacts concerning employment, and legal activity might be required. Safety policies being changed might result in a safer work environment or might result in a loophole being created that now allows for an unsafe condition. As with other changes that are made within the organization, data must be gathered to document a situation; then, based on that data, a new policy can be drafted that improves a condition of the current policy. This again is justified only based on measurements taken of a current policy that would justify a change to that policy. Developing a change process would also standardize the evaluation of policies, the change proposal process, the evaluation of risk process, and the capture and evaluation of data that justify change. Having this type of standard helps to control this area of the organization and control *who, what, when,* and *how* policy is changed if needed at all.

Documentation Changes

If not already established, a culture of documenting policies, procedures, and any records used throughout the organization should be developed. This would be in engineering, manufacturing, supply chain management, inventory control, accounting, and human resources.

Documentation is the written form of the establishment of the organization, policies, and procedures performed throughout the organization and is how standardization and control are established and maintained.

When an organization has developed a standardized process for documentation, it is then vitally important to establish a *change-control process*. This change process is vital because it controls how a document is updated and how updates are communicated to appropriate staff who would use that document. This is typically managed by someone or a department in charge of documentation control. Anyone proposing a change to a document would have to follow the established change-control process. Information required in the change process might include the following:

- Written description of the scope of change and why a change is necessary
- Statement of who is requesting the change
- Supporting documents or data that would illustrate what change is required

- List of who should evaluate, approve, and sign off on the proposed change

- List of people the change needs to be communicated to

Having this information forms the basis for what is needed to document, evaluate, and validate the change, as well as implement the elements called out in the change.

Power Tool

Having the *change-control process* established as a *standard* throughout the organization *promotes the consistency and control* necessary to maintain the quality of processes, procedures, and policies that will help ensure efficiencies within the organization.

Change as a Process

As we have seen with so many areas in the organization, processes are established to document, standardize, control, and communicate how tasks are to be carried out. Change is a task that organizations will have to implement and therefore should have an established process. When the process of change has been established, it can be used throughout the organization wherever change is needed. The organization might find they can establish one change process for documentation, but might have a slightly different process for changes in policies and procedures and yet another process best tailored for changing human resources or organizational structuring. Regardless of the level or type of change, a process should be established to document and control the steps required to implement the components of the change accomplishing the goal of that change.

There are four primary steps within the process of change: *propose, implement, communicate, and measure.*

1. Propose

- **Gather data**—The first step in determining whether a change is required is measuring what is currently being done. If this is organizational structure or depending on the type of business, this might be more a qualitative assessment that essentially documents where the organization currently stands. If this is a process or policy change, it can be quantified with actual data or measurements which indicate that change is necessary. This type of validation of change is only as good as the data that has been gathered. It is important to know that the entire change process starts with good and accurate data. This formulates the basis in justifying the change, as well as establishing the baseline for how to measure whether a change was actually successful.

- **Develop a business need**—After the appropriate data has been gathered and evaluated, it can be used to develop the details and scope of the change request. This is just as important as gathering correct data, because it summarizes what the data is actually indicating in a form that can be understood by those who will be evaluating the necessity of this change. When those evaluating the data see and understand the necessity of this change, it will then become a business need and will be justified as an improvement. This is a critical step in the change process; a business need should clearly be shown to justify the cost and logistics of implementing the change.

- **Propose change**—After the data has been gathered and a business need has clearly been identified, the change needs to be articulated and presented in the form of a proposal. This can be as simple as a short statement outlining the details of the change, called a change order process form, or can be as complex as an entire written proposal outlining all the details, including charts, graphs, and any other supporting drawings or documents required to articulate and illustrate the scope of the change. This is also important because this is how the details of the change will be communicated to those who will be signing off on the approval of this change. The importance is not only in the accuracy and completeness of data that was gathered, but also in the presentation of this data and in clearly showing what improvements the change is proposing to make.

- **Validate and sign off**—Proposed changes should be evaluated by those who have an interest in or some connection to the process being changed. For instance, a change to mid-level management structure would need to be evaluated by executive-level management to validate the business need. Likewise, changes to processes would need to be evaluated by those who created the process, those who are currently using the process, any applicable supporting staff such as quality or manufacturing engineers, as well as business managers who are familiar with the process and understand the impact of the proposed change. In the case of policies, appropriate department managers, human resources, safety committee, and executive staff or owners of organizations should validate both the need and the impact of the policy change.

The sign-off component is required not only in communicating a proposed change to those who might be affected by the change, but also in validating that the change will produce the desired outcome. This allows for more input on a change, possibly catching a flaw not seen by others, or making a slight modification that would ensure or enhance the success of the change. This is how change can be managed and controlled effectively to accomplish improvements, and eliminate as much risk as possible. This step should result in a sign-off by these individuals indicating that they have reviewed the details and scope of the change and approve of the steps that will be taken in implementing the change. This is a vital area in the change process, because it places the responsibility for this change on others qualified to make that judgment and not just the person requesting the change. This also shows that other interested parties or departments were involved in approving the change.

2. Implement

- **Conduct changes**—After the change has been signed off on and approved, the implementation process can begin. Implementing a change within the organization can be easy or difficult, depending on a number of situations. If those affected by the change know that the change is necessary, implementation of the change will be welcome because the improvements are needed. If the proposed change is not immediately recognized as a need, there might be some resistance by those not subscribing to the change or simply not understanding what improvement the change will result in. When changes are to be made, it's usually best to first communicate the intent and proposed outcome of a change because this can prepare the way for other steps in the implementation of that change.

  When changes are communicated in advance, this allows for questions to be answered and details to be shared that will help individuals understand the benefit and outcome of the change. This can also help to improve the general attitude of those affected by the change and possibly generate buy-in and participation in implementing the change. Because communication is important in many situations and at all levels in the organization, it is also important in implementing change.

- **Manage the scope of change**—When change is being implemented, it's important to note that the change was originally documented with very specific details as to what exactly needs to be changed. This is called the scope of the change and it defines the parameters surrounding only the things that need to be changed. It's important in the original proposal for specific details of the change to be outlined to establish the scope of the change so that when the change is implemented, only those things identified are allowed to be changed.

It's easy, during the implementation of change, to try to address other things not related to this change or expand the work of this change to alter things incorrectly and not as documented. This is why it's important for the change to be documented accurately and for those evaluating the change to certify that the change is valid given the details and the scope that was outlined in the document.

Part of the risk in making change is that the change might be done incorrectly, or more things might be changed than originally intended. It's the job of the person in charge of managing this change to manage the scope of the work being done in implementing the change. The manager of this change must also pay close attention to the details during the implementation to ensure that everything was carried out per the documented plan of this change. This is vital to the success of what this change intended to improve, to stay within the scope of the change and not create more problems than it solves.

- **Publicize changes**—When the implementation process is completed, the manager of this change should document that all steps have been completed and the process of this change has been verified. As with project management, the change process is much like a project in that there is a start, a finish, and a goal or a deliverable. It is important for the change process to have a definite finish to clarify that all requirements within the scope of the change have been fulfilled. It might be a requirement of the change process to have a final sign-off officially validating the completion of the change.

There might be other supporting documentation that will be generated, such as invoices, test results, or new drawings or illustrations, based on the new change, that will need to be issued to documentation control for update. This is also a vital step in the change process; although the change has been completed, all documents relative to that process still reflect the old way and need to be updated to reflect this change. This can be a form of communication indicating that something was changed and that the implementation is complete.

3. Communicate

- **Create a list of those who need to know**—Much like the beginning of the change process in which a group of individuals were identified as needing to evaluate the change, a list will also need to be generated which communicates that the change has been completed and is now in place. This should include the original group of those who evaluated the change at the beginning of the process, but should also include others such as departmental managers, executive management, or any supporting staff who will need to know that this change has been implemented.

  This is another important step in the change process because good communication saves the organization time and money in effectively communicating changes that are made throughout the organization. When something changes, it might or might not be visible to those in the surrounding area, but the outcome of what changed should be measurable in some way and therefore will be seen by someone. It is also important for people expecting an improvement to know that a change has been completed so that they know when to expect improvements to occur.

4. Measure

- **Go back to the original data**—It's the intent of change to make improvements and not to create adverse effects or be a burden on the organization. If data was taken at the beginning of this change that indicated there needed to be improvement, then that same data can be taken after the changes have been implemented to validate that the change was successful. This should be a requirement within the change process, to validate not only that the change was successful, but also that the invest-ment of resources and cost in the implementation of the change were justified.

  This will be part of the closure of this change, as well as the jus-tification for the change. This can also show that using a system-atic, organized process for change results in improvements that are controlled. This allows the organization to make changes at all levels, using data with either quantified or qualified assess-ment of risk, with some contingency planning and a measured outcome to verify success.

- **Determine whether it is sustainable**—The last part of changes made within the organization centers on the sus-tainability of the change after it has been implemented. This looks at the type of change that was made and the integrity of the approach at resolving an issue. Some changes might be simpler, as in documentation or policy changes that might sim-ply be reclarifying something or better articulating something that improves the quality of that policy or document. These changes are considered sustainable because they are clarifica-tion improvements.

  Changes in organizational structure might initially measure successful, but will require time to ensure that the change can maintain success given other organizational influences. It might be determined that further change might be required in the case of how the organization is divided up functionally and with certain leadership in place. It might also be determined that changes in departmental structure and/or leadership work well and will be very sustainable in both the short- and long-term, proving the success of the change.

In the case of processes and/or product development, these changes can be measured shortly after implementation as to whether they are successful. Process and product changes can be made as needed based on detailed and accurate monitoring that can produce real-time data indicating changes that need to be made. If this type of change is made, it can be measured and verified to validate sustainability.

As you have seen, change is inevitable within an organization and therefore it needs to be taken seriously by everyone in the organization. Change-control processes need to be developed and used throughout the organization to validate, to control implementation of, and to measure the success of changes that an organization needs to make. Changes can be a good thing if controlled and done correctly, but can be devastating if a process has not been developed to manage all the components of the change. Change is how organizations improve and stay competitive within their market, and when it is managed correctly, it allows organizations to maintain a competitive advantage.

Power Tool Summary

- When people see the *positive result* of an organized change-control process, they are *more comfortable in participating in change*!
- *Knowing the real data* associated with a proposed change *helps managers be more confident* in why changes are made and what the desired outcomes should be.

- It's the *development of the change process* that will help organize the components required in managing the implementation of change and ensure the success of change.

- Having the *change-control process* established as a *standard* throughout the organization *promotes the consistency and control* necessary to maintain the quality of processes, procedures, and policies that will help ensure efficiencies within the organization.

Bibliography

Barkley, Bruce. *Project Risk Management.* New York: McGraw-Hill, 2004. Print. 9780071436915

Bell, Arthur H., and Dayle M. Smith. *Management Communication.* Hoboken, NJ: Wiley, 2006. Print. 9780471755241

Boone, Louis E., and David L. Kurtz. *Contemporary Business.* Mason, OH: Thomson/South-Western, 2005. Print. 9780324188202

Cooper, Dale F. *Project Risk Management Guidelines: Managing Risk in Large Projects and Complex Procurements.* West Sussex, England: J. Wiley, 2005. Print. 9780470022818

Evans, James R., and William M. Lindsay. *Managing for Quality and Performance Excellence.* Mason, OH: Thomson/South-Western, 2008. Print. 9780324646856

Garrett, Gregory A. *World Class Contracting, Fifth Edition.* Chicago: CCH, 2007. Print. 9780808025689

Gray, Clifford F., and Erik W. Larson. *Project Management: The Managerial Process.* Boston: McGraw-Hill/Irwin, 2006. Print. 9780072978636

Griffin, Ricky W. *Management.* Boston: Houghton Mifflin, 2005. Print. 9780618354597

A Guide to the Project Management Body of Knowledge (PMBOK® Guide). Newtown Square, PA: Project Management Institute, 2008. Print. 9781933890517

Heizer, Jay H., and Barry Render. *Principles of Operations Management.* Upper Saddle River, NJ: Pearson/Prentice Hall, 2004. Print. 9780131016132

Heizer, Jay, and Barry Render. *Operations Management: Flexible Version.* Upper Saddle River, NJ: Pearson/Prentice Hall, 2007. Print. 9780132370608

Hiegel, James, Roderick James, and Frank Cesario. *Projects, Programs, and Project Teams: Advanced Program Management*. Hoboken, NJ: Wiley Custom Services, 2006. Print. 9780470037362

Jennings, Marianne. *Business: Its Legal, Ethical, and Global Environment*. Mason, OH: Thomson/South-Western, 2006. Print. 9780324204889

Kerzner, Harold. *Project Management: A Systems Approach to Planning, Scheduling, and Controlling*. Hoboken, NJ: Wiley, 2003. Print. 9780471225775

Lussier, Robert N., and Christopher F. Achua. *Leadership: Theory, Application, Skill Development*. Mason, OH: Thomson/South-Western, 2007. Print. 9780324316971

Nicholas, John M., and Herman Steyn. *Project Management for Business, Engineering, and Technology: Principles and Practice*. Amsterdam: Elsevier Butterworth Heinemann, 2008. Print. 9780750683999

Schermerhorn, John R., Richard Osborn, and James G. Hunt. *Organizational Behavior*. New York: Wiley, 2005. Print. 9780471681700

Schuyler, John R. *Risk and Decision Analysis in Projects*. Newtown Square, PA: Project Management Institute, 2001. Print. 9781880410288

Verma, Vijay K. *Organizing Projects for Success*. Upper Darby, PA: Project Management Institute, 1995. Print. 9781880410400

Verma, Vijay K. *Human Resource Skills for the Project Manager*. Newtown Square, PA: Project Management Institute, 1996. Print. 9781880410417

Index

FINANCIAL TIMES

In an increasingly competitive world, it is quality
of thinking that gives an edge—an idea that opens new
doors, a technique that solves a problem, or an insight
that simply helps make sense of it all.

We work with leading authors in the various arenas
of business and finance to bring cutting-edge thinking
and best-learning practices to a global market.

It is our goal to create world-class print publications
and electronic products that give readers
knowledge and understanding that can then be
applied, whether studying or at work.

To find out more about our business
products, you can visit us at www.ftpress.com.